I0828711

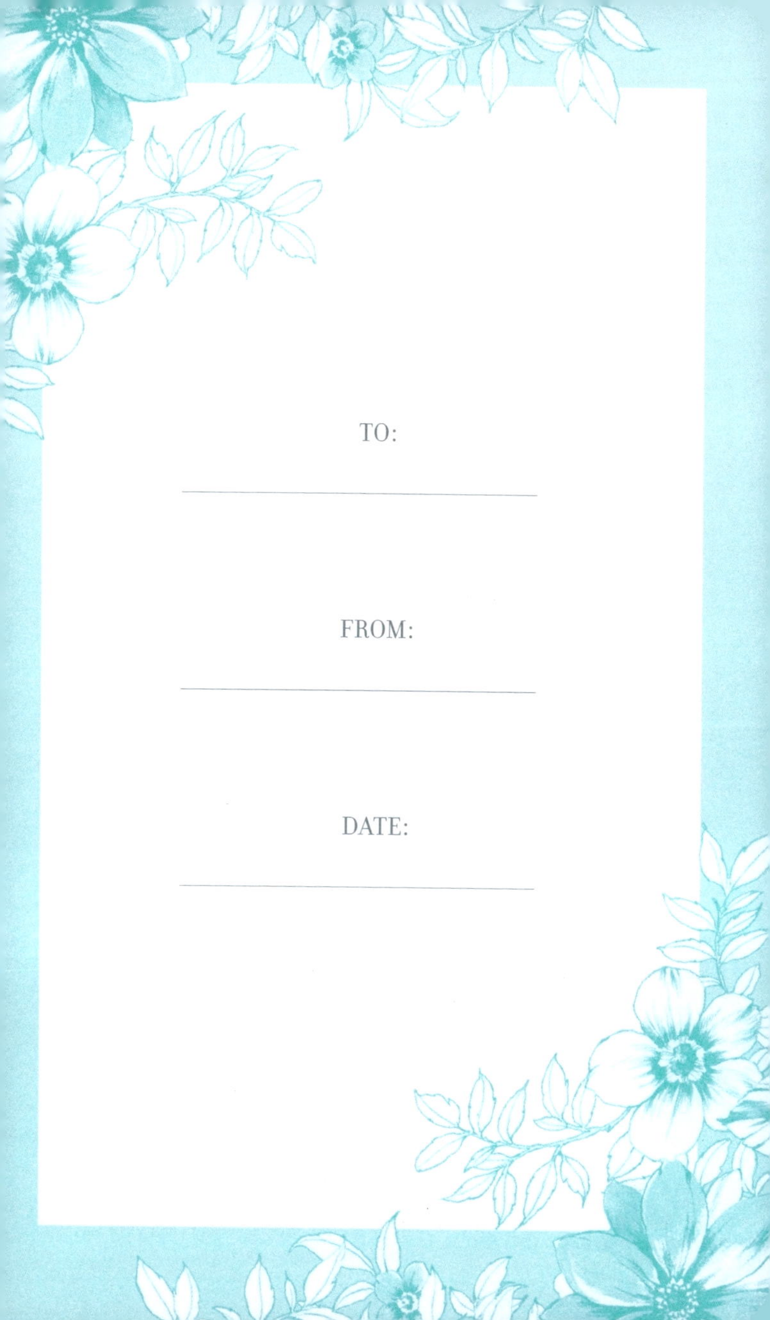

TO:

FROM:

DATE:

Visit Christian Art Gifts, Inc. at www.christianartgifts.com.

101 Prayers for Comfort in Difficult Times

Published by Christian Art Gifts Inc., IL, USA

Author is represented by the literary agency of Credo Communications LLC, Grand Rapids, Michigan, credocommunications.net.

Designed by Alyssa Montalto

Images used under license from Shutterstock.com

ISBN 978-1-63952-292-7

Printed in China

30 29 28 27 26 25
11 10 9 8 7 6 5 4 3 2

101 • PRAYERS FOR • COMFORT — IN — *Difficult Times*

KATE MOTAUNG

Christian Art
PUBLISHERS

Introduction

In times of crisis, hardship, and pain, it's so tempting to turn to the things of this world for help and relief. But inevitably, those so-called remedies are only temporary, and if we're honest, they only partially alleviate our distress. We need something greater, something more powerful. Something eternal.

As followers of Christ, we have access to a limitless fountain of comfort, hope, and peace through our intimate, personal relationship with the living God. Our Heavenly Father never runs out of grace, mercy, or love to shower on us in difficult times, and He never tires of hearing or answering our prayers according to His lovingkindness.

The God of all comfort invites us to come to Him, to call out to Him, to cast our cares on Him. In exchange, He promises to be our Prince of Peace, the Father of compassion, our ever-present help in times of trouble. As children of God, we need not fear or despair. We are held—firmly and securely—by the Lord of all creation, and no one is able to snatch us from His hand.

No matter what you may be going through, my hope is that these prayers will help you draw closer to the heart of Your God and King, and that you will sense His presence as you entrust your burdens into His capable arms.

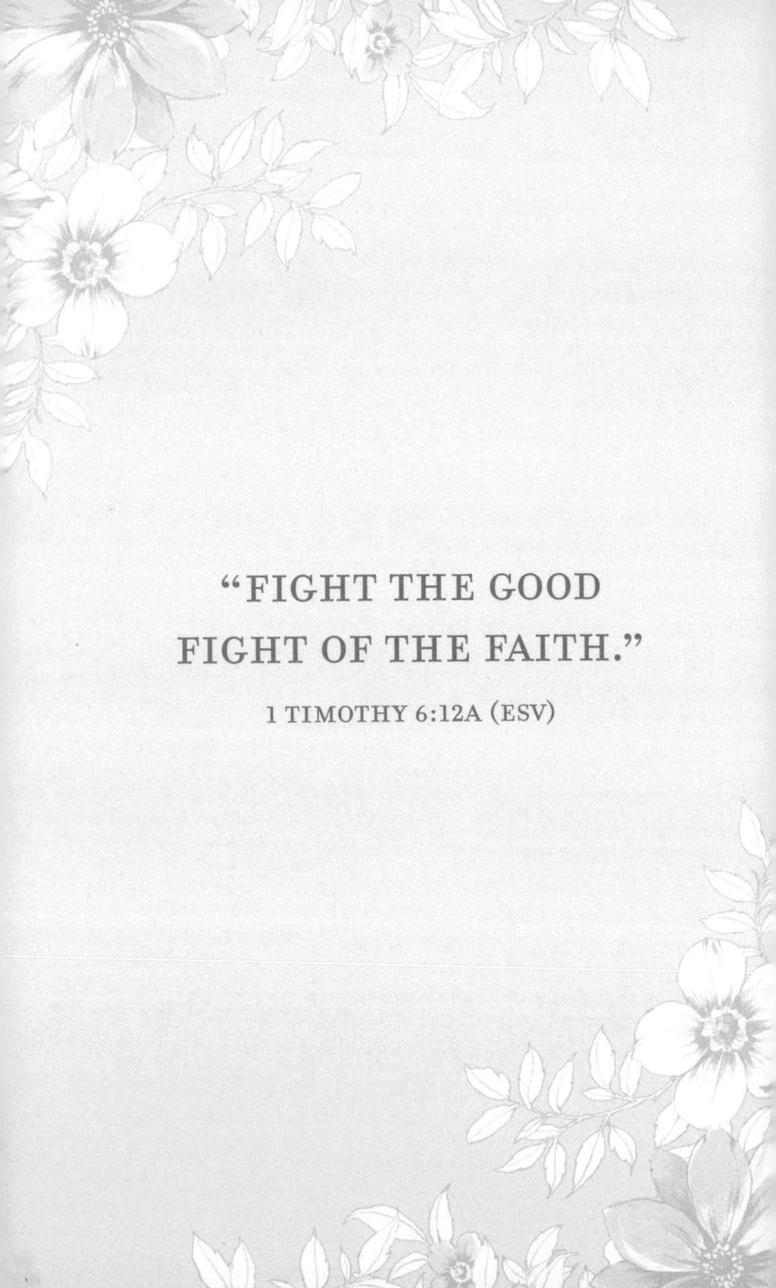

"FIGHT THE GOOD
FIGHT OF THE FAITH."

1 TIMOTHY 6:12A (ESV)

1

The God of All Comfort

"Blessed be the...God of all comfort, who comforts us in all our affliction, so that we may be able to comfort those who are in any affliction."

2 CORINTHIANS 1:3–4 (ESV)

Lord, You are the Father of mercies and the God of all comfort. It's who You are. You can't help Yourself. Thank You for comforting me in all my affliction—not only for my own benefit, but for the benefit of others as well.

Help me, Lord, to pay it forward. Keep me from holding an inward gaze that is focused only on myself. Open my eyes to see the needy and brokenhearted around me. Give me opportunities to use the grace and divine consolation I have received from You and pour it out on others who are hurting.

Grant me the boldness and generosity to give freely from what I have been given. Show me how to be Your hands and feet in this desperate world, for Your glory alone.

Amen

2

Compared to Christ

"Consider Him who endured such opposition from sinners, so that you will not grow weary and lose heart."

HEBREWS 12:3

Lord, I confess that I feel sorry for myself more often than I should. I fall to the temptation to pity my own circumstances and wallow in the weight of my sorrow. But the challenges I face are nothing compared to what Your Son, Jesus Christ, endured during His time on earth.

Forgive me for focusing on myself more than I look to You.

Make me grateful for all that Jesus suffered on my behalf. Give me eyes to see His endurance in the midst of opposition. Inspire me with His perfect example. Show me how to dwell on the person and work of Christ when I feel discouraged. Uplift me with thoughts of my Savior. When I am tempted to grow weary and lose heart, show me Jesus.

Lord, You alone are my portion and my strength, and I worship You.

Amen

3

He Goes Before You

"The Lord Himself goes before you and will be with you; He will never leave you nor forsake you."

DEUTERONOMY 31:8

Lord, You alone are faithful. You are my protector and deliverer. The promise of Your presence consoles me. Forgive me for the many times I have doubted Your nearness and questioned Your love.

When I feel lonely and fearful, God, remind me that You have never left me, You are with me now, and You will never abandon me in the future. I know I can rely on You and the trustworthiness of Your character. Whatever You declare is true.

Thank You for going before me, especially when the path ahead seems dark and ominous. Thank You for paving the way, for holding my hand, for staying by my side. Give me the trust and confidence of Paul, who wrote, "If God is for us, who can be against us?" (Romans 8:31). Truly, You are the greatest advocate of all.

Amen

4

A Heavenly Vision

"Set your minds on things above, not on earthly things."

COLOSSIANS 3:2

Lord, it's so easy for me to be nearsighted, to focus only on what is right in front of me in this moment. I get bogged down by my daily responsibilities and struggles and forget to consider the bigger picture.

Remind me to look up. Give me divine eyesight to gaze toward what lies ahead when You return. Show me how to set my mind on things above, not on earthly things. Grant me a burning desire to live for eternity, not just for this life.

Thank You that this life is not all that there is. Help me to find comfort in knowing that these trials will not last forever. One day You will wipe every tear from my eyes and take away every sorrow. Make me eager to be in Your presence, healed and whole.

Thank You for preparing a place for me in heaven with You (John 14:2-3).

Amen

5

My Only Help

"I lift up my eyes to the hills. From where does my help come? My help comes from the Lord, who made heaven and earth."

PSALM 121:1–2 (ESV)

Lord, I'm at the end of my rope. I've exhausted all of my usual resources. My strength is sapped. This trial has undone me.

Lift up my eyes to the heavens. Show me where my help comes from. Remind me that You are the only one who can carry me through this difficult season.

You knew about these circumstances before the beginning of time, and You are ready and willing to supply me with everything I need to persevere. You made the heavens and the earth; surely You can carry me through this trying time as well.

Forgive my lack of trust in You. Give me an added measure of faith in Your provision and character.

Grant me a voice to declare Your goodness to the world. Use this part of my story to magnify Your name.

Amen

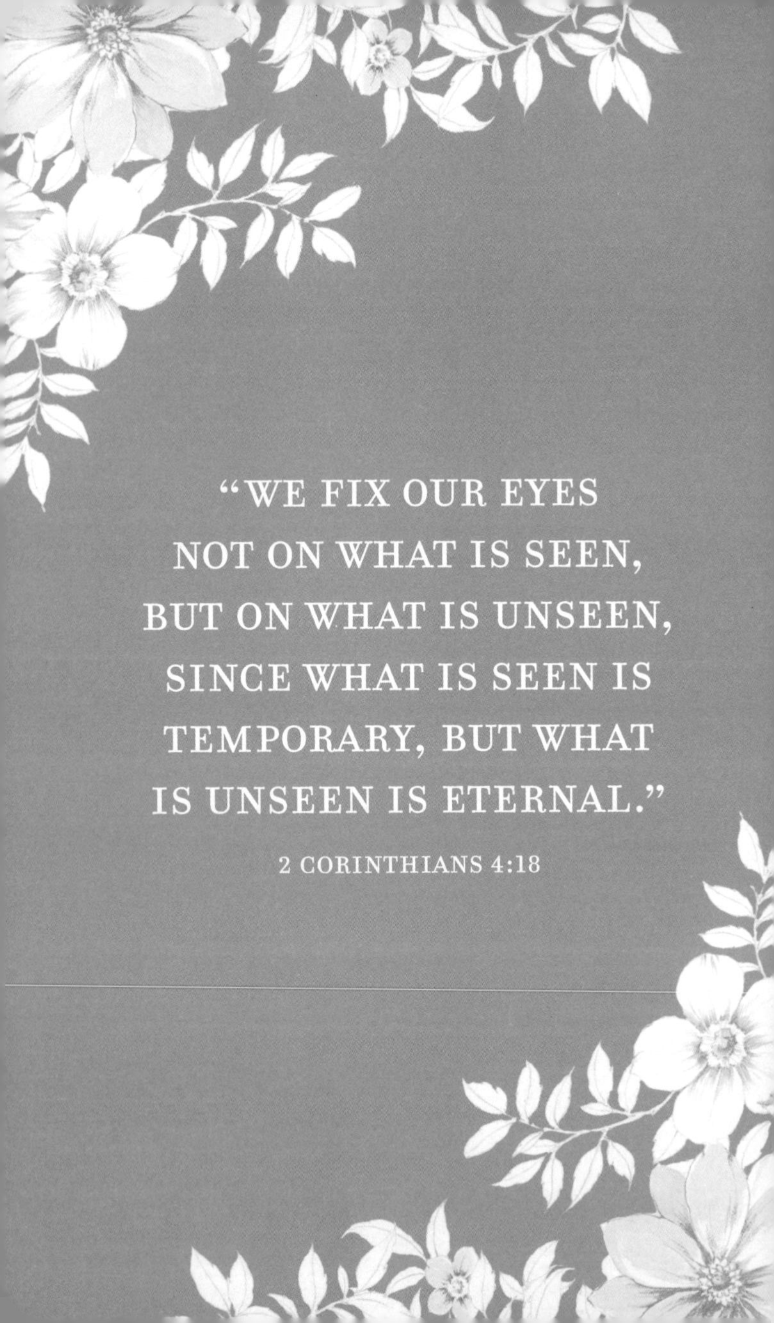

"WE FIX OUR EYES
NOT ON WHAT IS SEEN,
BUT ON WHAT IS UNSEEN,
SINCE WHAT IS SEEN IS
TEMPORARY, BUT WHAT
IS UNSEEN IS ETERNAL."

2 CORINTHIANS 4:18

6

Safe in His Constant Care

"He will not let your foot be moved;
He who keeps you will not slumber."

PSALM 121:3 (ESV)

Lord, thank You for being my security guard around the clock. Thank You for watching over me every moment of every day—even through the darkest watches of the night.

When I am struggling to sleep because of the sheer volume of cares and concerns swimming through my mind, remind me that You have it all taken care of already. You have a perfect plan and resolution, and my worry accomplishes nothing.

You are my faithful, capable Shepherd who cares for Your sheep and would lay down Your life for my sake.

I do not deserve You.

Thank You for ensuring that I will not slip and fall from Your grace. You promise that none can be snatched from Your hand (John 10:28-29). Comfort me with the realization that I cannot be harmed when I belong to You. You are my great protector.

Amen

7

Abundantly More

"Now to Him who is able to do far more abundantly than all that we ask or think...to Him be glory."

EPHESIANS 3:20A, 21A (ESV)

Lord, I confess that this situation seems impossible to resolve. I have lost hope of things ever getting better. Restoration seems unimaginable. It feels too late, too far gone to be redeemed.

I have been struggling to pray because I just don't think there is anything that can be done. I can't see a way out of this mess. It's a lost cause.

God, help me to believe that nothing is impossible with You (Luke 1:37).

Teach me to see and understand that there are no limits to what You are able to do. My finite mind cannot comprehend Your power. Give me the faith to ask, seek, and knock for more than I dare to think possible—according to Your will.

You are in the redemption business—You delight in making broken things whole. Thank You, Lord.

Amen

8

Companion for the Lonely

"And surely I am with you always, to the very end of the age."

MATTHEW 28:20B

Lord, I don't know why—and I don't even like to admit it—but I feel lonely. Even when I am surrounded by people, I still feel alone.

I know that because I am made in Your image, the image of the Triune God, You created me for connection and to be in relationship with others. Help me to find and invest in meaningful friendships—not to serve myself, but as a way to serve and be a blessing to others.

Keep me from searching for meaning or purpose in earthly relationships. Help me to find my identity in Christ. Whether I develop close friendships or not, remind me that You are with me *always*. There is never a moment that I am apart from You. Thank You for dwelling in me through Your Spirit. Help me to sense Your nearness to me when I feel alone.

Amen

9

He Sustains Me

"I lie down and sleep; I wake again, because the LORD sustains me."

PSALM 3:5

Lord, I have not been sleeping well. The circumstances in my life have kept me awake at night. When morning comes, I still feel tired instead of refreshed. This continual state of exhaustion is affecting my mental clarity and my ability to fulfill my responsibilities well.

Please grant me the sweet gift of rest. Help me not to take it for granted when sleep does come. Teach me how to quiet my mind and dwell on Your goodness instead of succumbing to the voices of worry.

Your mercies are new every morning (Lamentations 3:22-23). Give me a sense of gratitude when I wake up each new day, and remind me that You alone are sustaining me through every breath and moment.

You are a faithful God. Morning and evening, You never change. Your grace is sufficient for me. Show me my neediness and help me cling to You.

Amen

10

Calming the Storm

"He got up, rebuked the wind and said to the waves, 'Quiet! Be still!' Then the wind died down and it was completely calm."

MARK 4:39

Lord, thank You for the testimony of Your Word. I praise You for being the living Word who continues to speak into my life through timeless truth found in the Scriptures. Thank You for the many stories You have recorded for us of Your infinite power.

Just as Jesus rebuked the storm during His life on earth, I know that You are able to still the storm I am experiencing now. With a word, You could make it all go away and cause my life to be completely calm. But I am trusting that until You choose to do so, You have a purpose for this turbulent time. Use the wind and the waves in my life now to mold me into Your image. Help me cling to You as my anchor, I pray.

Amen

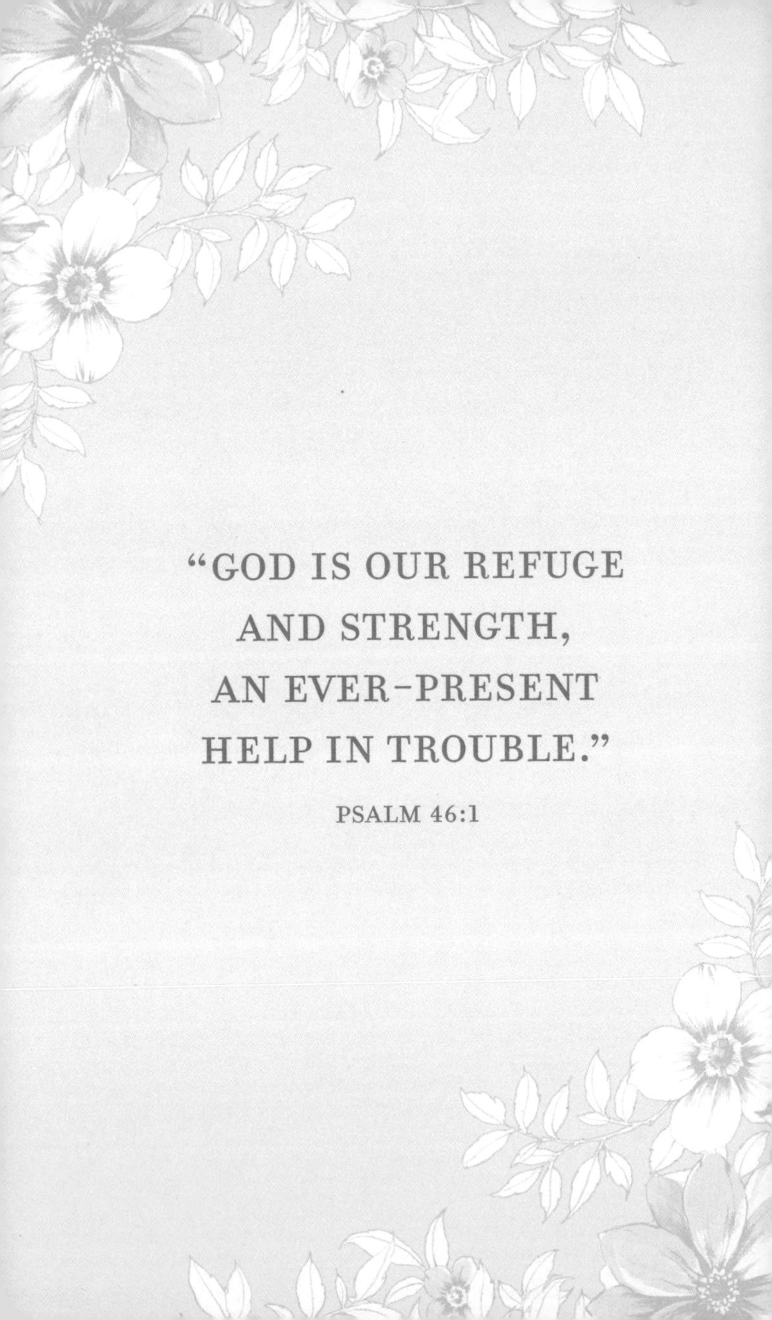

"GOD IS OUR REFUGE
AND STRENGTH,
AN EVER-PRESENT
HELP IN TROUBLE."

PSALM 46:1

11

Don't Be Surprised

"Do not be surprised at the fiery trial when it comes upon you to test you, as though something strange were happening to you."

1 PETER 4:12 (ESV)

Lord, thank You for the reminder that I should not be surprised by the trials that come in this life. After all, You did promise in Your Word, "In this world you will have trouble" (John 16:33). Thank You for not ending the promise there, but for reminding me to take heart because You have overcome the world.

Father, use these fiery trials to refine me and purify me. The sanctification process is often not pleasant at the time, but so necessary. Give me the grace to stand firm in my faith. Preserve my testimony for Your sake, I pray. Allow me to come through to the other side of this refining process looking more like Christ. Help me not to question You or Your ways, but to trust Your purposes.

Amen

12

My Dependable Rescuer

"He reached down from on high and took hold of me; He drew me out of deep waters."

2 SAMUEL 22:17

Lord, You are my rescuer. Whenever I feel like I am drowning, You are faithful to reach down and draw me out of the overwhelming flood. You always take notice of me. I know I don't deserve Your love, yet You care for me with compassion and tenderness.

I praise You for being the God who sees. Thank You for being my protector. I'm so grateful for the ways You have taught me that You are dependable. Thank You for revealing to me how much I desperately need You and Your grace.

Help me to testify of Your goodness before others. Give me a voice to speak of Your faithfulness. Use my rescue story to cause others to turn to You for mercy. You alone can save; You alone can rescue from the depths of darkness. You are my light and my salvation.

Amen

13

Hope in Grief

"We do not want you to be uninformed about those who sleep in death, so that you do not grieve like the rest of mankind, who have no hope."

1 THESSALONIANS 4:13

Lord, my heart is aching. My loss is great. Grief hurts more than I thought possible. And yet, I know that a day is coming when all will be made new. This is not the final chapter.

Lord, teach me how to grieve with hope. Show me what it means to process significant loss while still clinging to Your promises. In the midst of my brokenness, Lord, give me opportunities to testify to others about Your great and sacrificial love. Use my pain to increase my empathy for those around me who are also hurting. Your Word says that in all things You work for the good of those who love You (Romans 8:28)—even this. Take this part of my story and turn it into a testimony for good.

Amen

14

My Safe Hiding Place

"In the shadow of Your wings I will take refuge, till the storms of destruction pass by."

PSALM 57:1B (ESV)

Lord, You are my hiding place. Thank You for offering a safe refuge where I can tuck myself away for protection from this storm. Thank You for promising to care for me at all times. I praise You for Your persistent faithfulness, kindness, mercy, and grace.

When the world lets me down, I know I can run to You. When I feel attacked on every side, I know You are there for me, spreading out Your wings as a shield and shelter.

Help me to squash any fears that remain in my mind and heart. Teach me how to trust fully in Your perfect security. Give me the confidence and perspective of the psalmist who wrote, "The Lord is on my side; I will not fear. What can man do to me?" (Psalm 118:6). Thank You for being my strong defender.

Amen

15

A Plea for Wayward Loved Ones

"Rejoice in hope, be patient in tribulation, be constant in prayer."

ROMANS 12:12 (ESV)

Lord, my heart is weary from crying out to You for my lost family members. It seems as if nothing will ever change. They are far from You and don't respond to the truth of the gospel.

Show me how to rejoice in the hope that You know all things, that You have a plan, and that You are able to turn hearts of stone into hearts of flesh, for Your glory. Cause me to be patient in the midst of this trial and heartache. Give me the grace to rest in Your perfect timing. Grant me the stamina to be constant and persistent in prayer and not to lose hope.

Teach me how to be a bright light that attracts others to the light of Christ. Keep me from doing any damage to Your name—intentionally or unintentionally. Use Your Spirit to draw wayward hearts to Yourself.

Amen

"LEAD ME TO
THE ROCK THAT IS
HIGHER THAN I."

PSALM 61:2B

16

Defeating Discontentment

"Keep your life free from love of money, and be content with what you have, for He has said, 'I will never leave you nor forsake you.'"

HEBREWS 13:5 (ESV)

Lord, You have given me so much. I have more than I deserve in Christ. You are a generous God, abundant in Your provision and care for me.

The world bombards me with messages telling me I need more, urging me to want more. My flesh is weak, and I give in to the lie that I don't have enough. Forgive me for all the times I have been discontent. Guard my heart from the love of money. Help me to resist the temptation to covet. Remind me that You always give me exactly what I need to make me more like Your Son.

Lord, make me fully and completely content with the wonder of Your constant presence. I have You, and that means I have all that I need. You are enough for me.

Amen

17

Sufficient Strength

"The bolts of your gates will be iron and bronze, and your strength will equal your days."

DEUTERONOMY 33:25

Lord, help me to cling to the truths and promises of Your Word. Thank You for promising that You will supply sufficient strength for each day that You give me. With You, I will always have enough energy to accomplish the tasks You set before me to do.

Not only do you provide physical strength, but also mental, emotional, and spiritual stamina. You care about every aspect of my being.

Your reserves of grace never run out; the well of Your mercy constantly overflows. I praise You for being Jehovah Jireh, the God who will provide.

Lord, thank You for protecting me from my enemies—even those I cannot see. You never stop watching over me, and You will not allow darkness to prevail.

As You give me the endurance to persevere, help me to testify to the source of my strength—You and You alone.

Amen

18

Counted Worthy

"The apostles left the Sanhedrin, rejoicing because they had been counted worthy of suffering disgrace for the name."

ACTS 5:41

Lord, I have faced opposition for exalting the name of Christ. I've been treated poorly because of my faith. Others don't understand. They tease, mock, and ridicule. I'm tempted to shrink back; cause me to stand firm in defense of the cross.

Give me the confidence and boldness to declare like the Apostle Paul, "I am not ashamed of the gospel" (Romans 1:16).

Remind me of these words of Christ: "Everyone who acknowledges me before men, I also will acknowledge before my Father who is in heaven, but whoever denies me before men, I also will deny before my Father who is in heaven" (Matthew 10:32-33, ESV).

Lord, my heart's desire is to be an acknowledger of You and not a denier. Equip me with Your Spirit to be Your witness. Help me to sincerely rejoice in the honor of being counted worthy.

Amen

19

Dealing with Disappointment

"Hope deferred makes the heart sick."

PROVERBS 13:12A (ESV)

Lord, my heart is sick from disappointments. I let myself get my hopes up, and the plans did not materialize. Deferred again. I feel it in my body, the ache and weariness of being let down. I am hesitant to allow myself to look forward to anything in the future for fear that I will just be hurt once more.

Father, help me to trust in Your perfect plan. Help me to believe that You have allowed this disappointment to happen for a reason—even for my good. Use this deferred dream to redirect my heart and mind to Your goodness, kindness, and mercy. I know that You only do what is best for me, even though I may not understand how or why. Give me the grace to rely on Your purposes even when I can't comprehend them.

Lord, strengthen my hope for eternity with You—a hope that far surpasses any earthly desire.

Amen

20

A Spiritual Battle

"Put on the whole armor of God, that you may be able to stand against the schemes of the devil."

EPHESIANS 6:11(ESV)

Lord, Your Word says that my "struggle is not against flesh and blood, but against the rulers, against the authorities, against the powers of this dark world and against the spiritual forces of evil in the heavenly realms" (Ephesians 6:12).

Since this battle is not an earthly one, I desperately need Your divine assistance. Clothe me with Your armor, Lord, with the belt of truth, the breastplate of righteousness, the shield of faith, the helmet of salvation, the sword of the Spirit, and ready feet (see Ephesians 6:14-17).

Show me the ways in which I'm relying on unreliable weapons and trusting in worthless idols. Help me to identify and stand against the devil's schemes when they come. Remind me that this is a spiritual war and that I need Your Holy Spirit to fight for me. You are my defender.

Amen

“BECAUSE OF THE LORD’S GREAT LOVE WE ARE NOT CONSUMED, FOR HIS COMPASSIONS NEVER FAIL. THEY ARE NEW EVERY MORNING; GREAT IS YOUR FAITHFULNESS.”

LAMENTATIONS 3:22–23

21

Assurance of Forgiveness

"If we confess our sins, He is faithful and just to forgive us our sins and to cleanse us from all unrighteousness."

1 JOHN 1:9 (ESV)

Lord, I confess that I struggle with feelings of guilt and shame over past sins. I'm so embarrassed by my former actions and grieved that I have offended You and Your holy law. I frequently dwell on what I have done.

Thank You for Your promise of forgiveness. I'm so grateful for Your purifying grace. I praise You for Your finished work on the cross. Thank You that my salvation does not depend on me, but solely on the paid sacrifice of Jesus Christ.

Help me to wholeheartedly accept and embrace Your offer of complete forgiveness. Show me how to live my life in gratitude as a forgiven sinner. I know I will continue to struggle, but Your grace is abundant and sufficient. Thank You for covering me and my shame with Your cleansing blood. I love You, Lord.

Amen

22

Fighting Fear

"When I am afraid, I will trust in You."

PSALM 56:3

Lord, help me to commit this verse to memory and recite it whenever I am tempted to fear: "When I am afraid, I will trust in You." At night, in the morning, and throughout the day, help me to replace fear with faith. Cause my trust in You to prevail over the frequent urges to worry.

You are my constant rock, my faithful friend, my firm foundation. You are my refuge and my strength, my ever-present help in trouble (see Psalm 46:1). You will never let me down.

Thank You for being a safe place that I can always turn to in times of need. Wash the worries away with the cleansing power of Your truth. Remind me of my position as Your beloved child. You wrap Your loving arms around me and shield me from the enemy. The victory is already Yours in Christ. I have no reason to be afraid.

Amen

23

Gratitude in the Dark

*"Give thanks in all circumstances,
for this is God's will for you in Christ Jesus."*

1 THESSALONIANS 5:18

Lord, in the midst of this trial, it's hard for me to be thankful. And yet Your Word says I should give thanks in *every* circumstance, not just the easy or positive ones. Train my mind, heart, and soul to practice gratitude as naturally as I breathe.

Even though this valley is dark, help me to see Your hand at work. Thank You for giving me breath. Thank You for not abandoning me in this dark place. Thank You for hearing my prayers. Thank You for new mercies every morning. Thank You for Your sufficient grace for each moment. Thank You for the gift of Your Son and His redeeming work on the cross. Thank You for the promise of His return. Thank You for the hope of a renewed body in the next life. Thank You for the anticipation of glory with You.

Amen

24

He Will Deliver Us

"He delivered us from such a deadly peril, and He will deliver us. On Him we have set our hope that He will deliver us again."

2 CORINTHIANS 1:10 (ESV)

Lord, You are the great deliverer. The Bible is filled with story after story of Your miraculous, wonderful deliverance of Your children. You parted the Red Sea for Your people to cross over to safety. You sent manna and quail in the desert.

You caused Goliath to fall at the hands of a shepherd boy with a stone. You tore down the walls of Jericho. You spared Moses and Joseph and Rahab from certain death. The list goes on and on. You are in the business of delivering. Past, present, and future—you have delivered, you are delivering, and You will deliver again.

On You I set my hope that You will also rescue me from this trial according to Your gracious will. Give me a holy confidence and patience to wait on You.

Amen

25

Healing from Sickness

"Bless the Lord, O my soul, and forget not all His benefits, who forgives all your iniquity, who heals all your diseases."

PSALM 103:2–3 (ESV)

Lord, You already know I don't feel well. You created my inmost being. You knit me together in my mother's womb (Psalm 139:13). Because You made me and have power even over death, I know You are able to fix whatever is wrong with my body. Please restore my health according to Your will.

Give me patience to endure this physical suffering. I know it is only temporary and that one day I will be made whole. I pray that You would use this weakness and frailty in my body to gain glory for Yourself. Show me how to use this part of my story as a testimony of Your goodness and mercy.

Thank You for sustaining me. Please grant me new mercies every morning and help me to lean on You. I am weak, but You are strong.

Amen

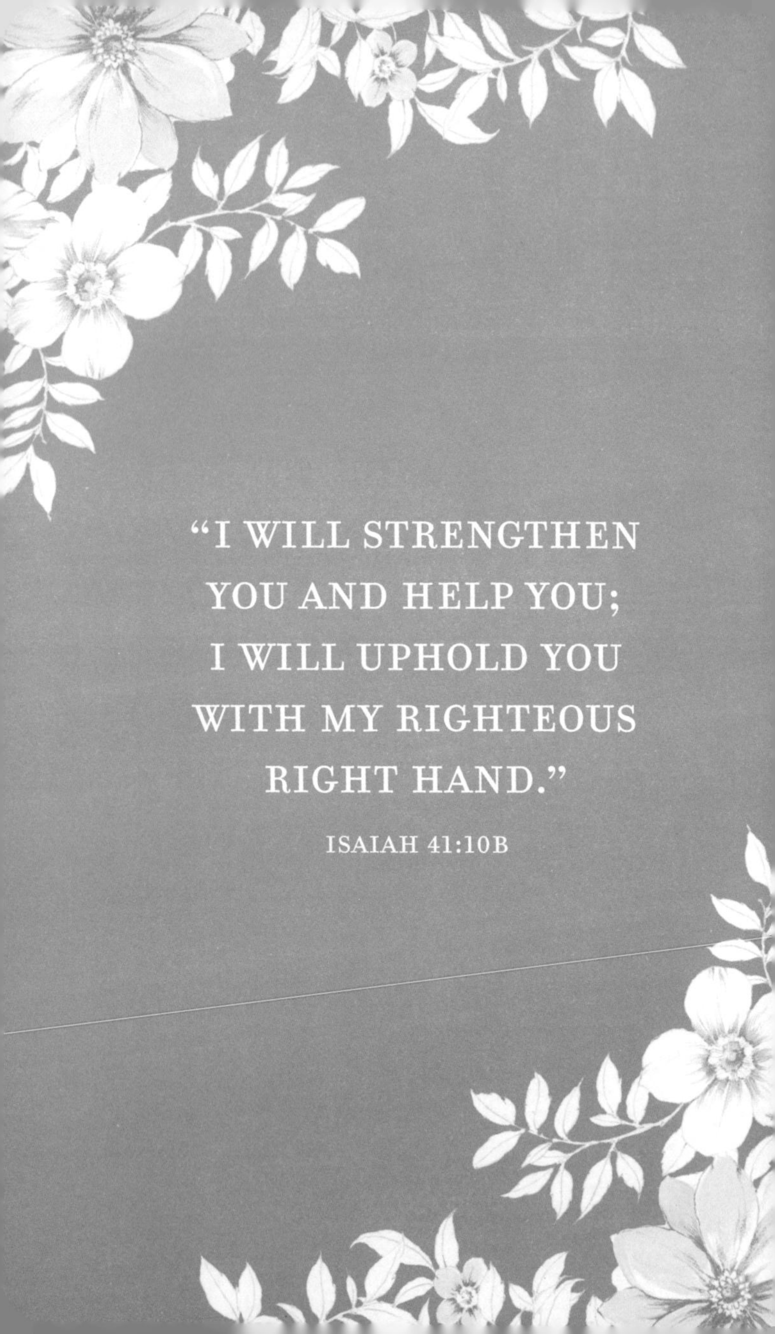
“I WILL STRENGTHEN
YOU AND HELP YOU;
I WILL UPHOLD YOU
WITH MY RIGHTEOUS
RIGHT HAND.”
ISAIAH 41:10B

26

Purposeful Thoughts

"Whatever is true, whatever is noble, whatever is right, whatever is pure, whatever is lovely, whatever is admirable—if anything is excellent or praiseworthy—think about such things."

PHILIPPIANS 4:8

Lord, I confess that I often let my mind wander down unhelpful paths that lead me away from trusting in You. I get caught up in worry, fear, anger, bitterness, jealousy, comparison, discontentment, and so much more. Particularly when I'm facing hardships, it's so easy for me to focus on the negative aspects of my circumstances instead of clinging to hope.

Train my mind to be set on You. Teach me to lay aside thoughts that do not bring You glory and instead to dwell on what is good. Help me to discern between truth and error. Turn my mind and heart quickly back to You when I begin to go astray.

Help me to take each thought captive and make it obedient to Christ (see 2 Corinthians 10:5). Fill me with Your Spirit.

Amen

If God Is for Us

"With Your help I can advance against a troop; with my God I can scale a wall."

2 SAMUEL 22:30

Lord, with You by my side, I can do anything according to Your will and by the power of Your Spirit. You've proven in Your Word that You can send legions of angels with a single word. You can still a raging storm. You can fell a whole army with a breath. If God is for me, who can be against me? (see Romans 8:31).

I confess that sometimes I grow discouraged by the walls, mountains, and enemies that lie ahead of me. The task seems insurmountable. And it is—on my own. But "with God all things are possible" (Matthew 19:26b).

Thank You for equipping me with Your supernatural strength. Your grace is sufficient for me (see 2 Corinthians 12:9). Help me to stop relying on my own efforts and instead lean on You for every next step.

Amen

28

The Father's Pleasure

"Do not be afraid, little flock, for your Father has been pleased to give you the kingdom."

LUKE 12:32

Lord, thank You for encouraging me not to be afraid. Help me to find peace in You. I'm so grateful that You made me part of Your flock. You are a good and faithful Shepherd who cares for my every need. Help me to follow Your lead and accept Your gentle correction.

Thank You for allowing me to call You Father. It's a privilege to be counted as one of Your children; help me not to take this amazing relationship for granted. I praise You for being a generous God. You take pleasure in giving the best to Your children. Thank You for reminding me that the best gifts are not material, temporary things. You give me so much more—gifts that will not deteriorate or be destroyed, but eternal gifts that will last forever. Help me to steward these gifts well for Your glory.

Amen

29

Life Transitions

"And He made from one man every nation of mankind to live on all the face of the earth, having determined allotted periods and the boundaries of their dwelling place."

ACTS 17:26 (ESV)

Lord, I'm facing another season of uncertainty. It seems You continue to give me opportunities to be reminded that I'm not in control, and I don't know what the future holds. Thank You for being the one in control of it all, the one who has known every next step and every bend in the road from before You created time.

Thank You that Your Word says You already knew and determined in advance where I would live, when, and for how long. Help me to stay attentive to Your lead and to rest in Your arms as You carry me through this winding path called life. Even though I have no idea what's coming next, I know that I will be held.

With Your help, I will follow You.

Amen

30

Overcoming Anxiety

"Cast all your anxiety on Him because He cares for you."

1 PETER 5:7

Lord, I confess that I have been anxious about many things. I realize that my fears only reflect my lack of trust in You. Forgive me, Lord. "I believe; help my unbelief!" (Mark 9:24, ESV).

I know that You really do care for me. Sometimes I don't understand why, but I trust that You do. Thank You for Your constant concern and love. Help me to meditate on Your unchanging attributes. You are compassionate and merciful. You are faithful and just. You are almighty and all-knowing. You are a forgiving God. You are patient. You are good. You are love.

When I dwell on Your character, my heart is calmed and my fears are reduced, knowing that I have an all-powerful God on my side who will fight for me, who cares intimately for me and my well-being, and who desires my good. I cannot thank You enough.

Amen

"WE ARE HARD PRESSED
ON EVERY SIDE,
BUT NOT CRUSHED;
PERPLEXED, BUT NOT IN
DESPAIR; PERSECUTED,
BUT NOT ABANDONED;
STRUCK DOWN,
BUT NOT DESTROYED."

2 CORINTHIANS 4:8–9

31

Bless His Name

"The Lord gave, and the Lord has taken away; blessed be the name of the Lord."

JOB 1:21B (ESV)

Lord, sometimes this life feels like one loss after another. There is so much pain, heartache, and grief—personally, locally, nationally, and globally. I've lost the desire to read the notifications on my phone, open my email, or turn on the radio or TV because I'm not sure I can stomach any more bad news. It seems as if I am constantly losing opportunities, dreams, possessions, relationships, and loved ones. It hurts, God.

Thank You for providing a safe space where I can mourn, grieve, and lament. Help me to accept these losses as part of Your overarching plan for my life to mold me and shape me into Your likeness. Help me to praise You in times of plenty and times of want. Whether You give or take away, give me the grace to bless Your name. You are a good Father, and I love You.

Amen

32

My Unchanging God

"Jesus Christ is the same yesterday and today and forever."

HEBREWS 13:8

Lord, the uncertainty of this life is unnerving. It seems as if every day brings new, unexpected challenges. I never know what's waiting for me around the next bend in the road, and my body feels anxious and on edge. I want to rest in Your presence, but my fears of the future continually elbow their way past my attempts to experience peace.

In the midst of continual change, I'm grateful that I can rely on Your unchanging nature and character. Thank You for being the same yesterday, today, and forever. I praise You for being my constant, ever-present help in times of need. I give You the glory for being my stable Rock when it feels as if the foundation might crumble beneath me.

Help me to stand firm on the foundation of Your Word. Lead me to trust You without faltering by the help of Your Holy Spirit.

Amen

33

Constant Provision

"The jar of flour was not used up and the jug of oil did not run dry, in keeping with the word of the Lord spoken by Elijah."

1 KINGS 17:16

Lord, I confess that, in my weakness, I have doubted Your willingness and ability to provide. My lack has overshadowed my faith, and I have feared not having enough. Instead of turning to You in prayer and dependence, I have turned to the frantic voices of worry in my head.

God, You can do anything. Nothing is too difficult for You. Your wonders are magnificent, Your miracles never ending. You can nourish thousands with just a few loaves and fish, and still have food leftover (see Matthew 14:13-21). You are a God of abundance, not scarcity. You invite me to ask, seek, and knock (see Matthew 7:7-8). You know my needs, Lord. You are a loving Father who gives good gifts to His children. Multiply the flour and oil, I pray.

Amen

34

Financial Hardship

"My God will supply every need of yours according to His riches in glory in Christ Jesus."

PHILIPPIANS 4:19 (ESV)

Lord, I confess that I am nervous. I don't know how I'm going to make it financially. No matter how many times I check the bank statement or calculate the numbers, I just can't see how I'm going to make ends meet. It's a scary position to be in, Lord. I feel desperate.

Help me to trust in Your provision. Remind me of the countless ways You have shown Your faithfulness over the years. You know my needs before I do, and You hear my pleas for help. Guide my prayers to align with Your will, God, and give me the strength to trust in You for my every need. I know You care for me. Forgive me for my doubt and unbelief. Give me opportunities to praise You in times of plenty and times of want. You are a good, good Father.

Amen

35

Determined to Hope

"Why, my soul, are you downcast?
Why so disturbed within me? Put your hope in God,
for I will yet praise Him, my Savior and my God."

PSALM 42:5

Lord, I've been struggling with my emotions lately. I feel so down and discouraged, day and night. I lack energy and motivation. A dark cloud lingers overhead, and I can't see the light or enjoy the warmth of Your smile toward me. All of my thoughts are negative and depressing.

Thank You for seeing my heart and hearing my lament. Like the psalmist, help me to determine to hope in You. You are my Savior and my God; deepen my faith to praise You even in the midst of this valley.

Even if the darkness persists, I pray that You would protect my testimony. Turn my heart toward You and not away from You. "You are my Lord; apart from You I have no good thing" (Psalm 16:2). You are my anchor.

Amen

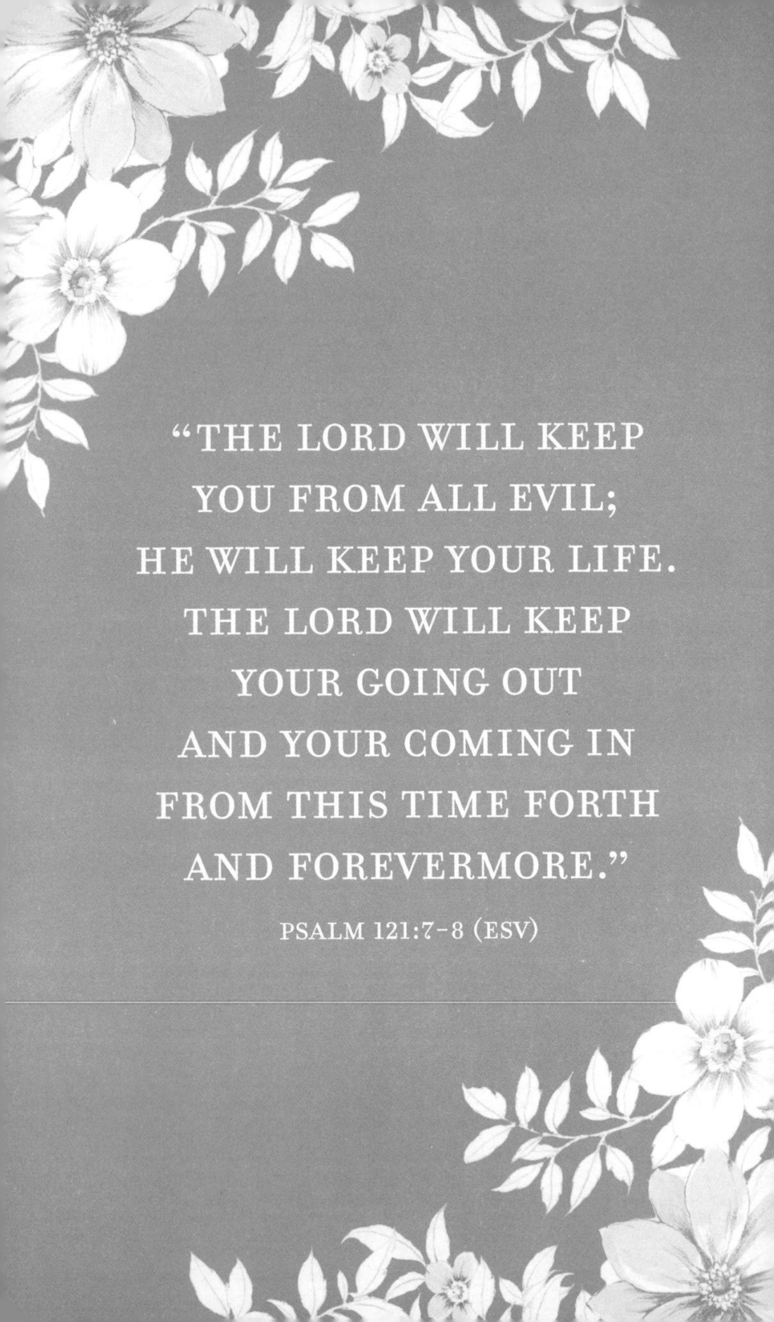
"THE LORD WILL KEEP
YOU FROM ALL EVIL;
HE WILL KEEP YOUR LIFE.
THE LORD WILL KEEP
YOUR GOING OUT
AND YOUR COMING IN
FROM THIS TIME FORTH
AND FOREVERMORE."
PSALM 121:7–8 (ESV)

36

A Way of Escape

"No temptation has overtaken you that is not common to man."

1 CORINTHIANS 10:13A (ESV)

Lord, I feel as if I'm under attack. I know that my "struggle is not against flesh and blood, but against the rulers, against the authorities, against the powers of this dark world and against the spiritual forces of evil in the heavenly realms" (Ephesians 6:12).

Give me the strength to resist the devil. Cause him to flee from me, in Jesus' name (see James 4:7).

Thank You for the comforting assurance that this trial is not new or exclusive to me. Thank You for promising not to let me be tempted beyond my ability in Christ. Thank You for always providing a way of escape and for enabling me to endure it (see 1 Corinthians 10:13).

Deliver me from this temptation. Empower me to use the escape route and not avoid it. Keep me from sinning against You. Protect my testimony for Your name's sake.

Amen

37

The Great Deliverer

"Then they cried out to the Lord in their trouble, and He brought them out of their distress."

PSALM 107:28

Lord, You are the great Deliverer. As Simon Peter answered when Your Son asked if the disciples were going to leave as well, "Lord, to whom shall we go? You have the words of eternal life" (John 6:68). There is no one else like You, no one else I can cry out to when I am in trouble. You alone can rescue me from my distress.

Thank You for hearing me when I cry to You. Even when I can't hear or sense Your response immediately, I know You are the God who hears and answers according to Your perfect will. Even if the rescue doesn't come in the way or timing I expect, I know that You will deliver me—if only on the last day. You have already claimed the victory, and I place my trust in You alone.

Amen

38

Rely on God

"We were so utterly burdened beyond our strength that we despaired of life itself... But that was to make us rely not on ourselves but on God."

2 CORINTHIANS 1:8B–9 (ESV)

Lord, this passage above describes how I feel right now. Utterly burdened beyond my strength. Despairing of life itself. Staring down a death sentence.

But God.

Could it be that You have allowed these circumstances precisely to reveal my desperate need of You? Could it be that I have been trusting in my own strength for too long? Could it be that I have been depending on myself to make it through the day, the week, the month, the year?

But God.

You do not leave me to despair. Through Your work on the cross, You have not left me without a way of escape. You raise the dead, and You have promised to raise me out of this pit in Your perfect timing to eternal life with You. I can't thank You enough.

Amen

39

The Truth About Jealousy

*"A tranquil heart gives life to the flesh,
but envy makes the bones rot."*

PROVERBS 14:30 (ESV)

Lord, I confess that I have been struggling with jealousy, and it's eating away at me from the inside. My bitterness is only affecting me negatively; there is no benefit to it.

I realize that the root of my envy is discontentment and covetousness. Forgive me for not being grateful for exactly what You have given me. I have no right to lust for more; You have given me far more than I deserve. Silence the voices that tempt me to compare myself and my situation with others, to want what they have.

"Create in me a clean heart, O God, and renew a right spirit within me" (Psalm 51:10, ESV). Purify me from my sinful desires. Open my eyes to see the depth of Your generosity. Overwhelm me with a lasting sense of gratitude for all that You have done for me through Christ.

Amen

40

My All-Knowing Father

"Your Father knows what you need before you ask Him."

MATTHEW 6:8

Lord, thank You for inviting me to come to You in prayer. I praise You for hearing me and answering me according to Your will. I'm so grateful that You desire a relationship with me. Forgive me for taking You for granted and not seeking Your face as often as I should.

You are omnipresent and all-knowing. You have known everything about me since before I was created. You knit me together in my mother's womb. You know every hair on my head. I believe You want what's best for me, even if I don't always understand Your purposes.

Help me to align my prayers to Your will and trust that You are working all things for my good—even when it doesn't make sense. I may not get the answers I desire in this lifetime, but I trust that You are a good God, and You care for me.

Amen

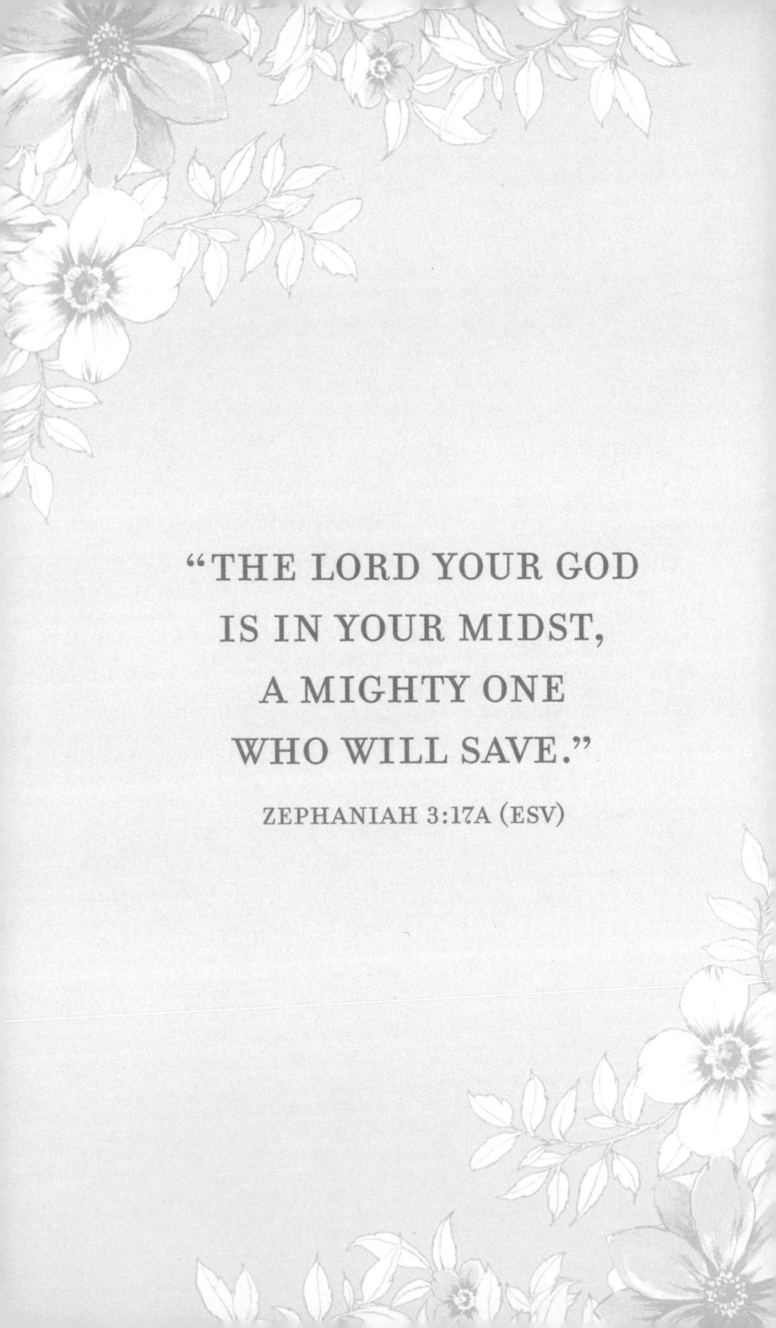

"THE LORD YOUR GOD
IS IN YOUR MIDST,
A MIGHTY ONE
WHO WILL SAVE."

ZEPHANIAH 3:17A (ESV)

41

Antidote for Discouragement

"He brought me out into a spacious place;
He rescued me because He delighted in me."

2 SAMUEL 22:20

Lord, I'm feeling very low today. I can't put my finger on the reason exactly—perhaps the heaviness of the ongoing burdens in my life is weighing me down.

I have so much to be grateful for; help me to resist this looming sense of discouragement. Lift my eyes to see the big picture. Show me the expanse of Your goodness. Remind me of the wonder of Your rescue. Give me a glimpse of Your smile to reveal Your delight in me.

I don't deserve Your grace or Your love, Lord, yet You are so kind to me. Thank You for all that You have done for me through Your Son on the cross and through the sustaining work of Your Holy Spirit in me. Forgive me for my ingratitude and discontentment. Lead me to live with lavish exuberance for Your presence in my life.

Amen

42

Workplace Woes

*"And whatever you do, whether in word or deed,
do it all in the name of the Lord Jesus,
giving thanks to God the Father through Him."*

COLOSSIANS 3:17

Lord, I'm struggling at my job. Things are challenging and seem to be getting worse. I know I should be grateful that I have work at all, but it takes such an effort just to leave the house in the mornings and make it through each day. I question why I'm there at all, what purpose I'm serving.

Help me to find ways to glorify You in the midst of my workdays. Give me reasons to find joy. Show me how I can be a light in the workplace even when I don't feel like it. Open doors for meaningful conversations with my colleagues that could have an eternal impact. Father, help me to work for You above all and to find my hope and purpose in serving You as my ultimate Master and Lord.

Amen

43

Persistent Rescue

"David said, 'The Lord who delivered me from the paw of the lion and from the paw of the bear will deliver me from the hand of this Philistine.'"

1 SAMUEL 17:37 (ESV)

Lord, You have rescued me so many times in the past; I cannot even count them. Thank You for continually saving me from a whole host of dangers and snares.

Now, as I face a challenge that seems greater than all the others, I pray that You would remind me of Your unfailing faithfulness in the past. You always keep Your promises. Give me an unfaltering confidence in Your character—You are who You say You are, and there is none like You.

Though this obstacle is far larger than I can conquer on my own, I know that You are with me and You will deliver me. You have the power to help me overcome in Your timing and according to Your perfect will. Thank You for loving me.

Amen

Inward Renewal

"We do not lose heart. Though outwardly we are wasting away, yet inwardly we are being renewed day by day."

2 CORINTHIANS 4:16

Lord, I confess that it is so easy for me to focus on my outward circumstances. I feel like I am wasting away. I am weak; my physical strength is failing me. Yet, I cling to You with everything I have left.

Please don't allow me to lose heart or grow discouraged in the midst of this trial. Show me glimpses of the inward work that only You can accomplish in me. Remind me that Your Spirit is renewing me day by day.

Help me to be a light and a testimony of Your grace to others who see me enduring this struggle. Prevent me from claiming any of the credit for myself, for You alone can do this.

Keep me in Your Word; help me to hide it in my heart. You are my life. Draw me close, I pray.

Amen

45

The Aftermath of Trauma

"Have no fear of sudden disaster...for the Lord will be at your side and will keep your foot from being snared."

PROVERBS 3:25A–26

Lord, I don't know what's wrong with me. My heart is consumed with irrational fear. I know the truth in my mind and heart, but my body is not cooperating. Unexpected triggers lead to unbidden physical reactions. I wish I could make it go away.

Please heal me from the aftermath of the trauma I have experienced. Restore healthy responses in my brain, heart, breath, and limbs. Grant me patience as You work and use this for my good.

Father, You are my defender. Shield me from the fear of sudden disaster. Assure me of the consistency of Your presence. Show me Your footprints in the sand as You carry me.

Thank You for keeping my foot from being snared. I pray that You would remind me each moment that Jesus Himself is my peace (see Ephesians 2:14).

Amen

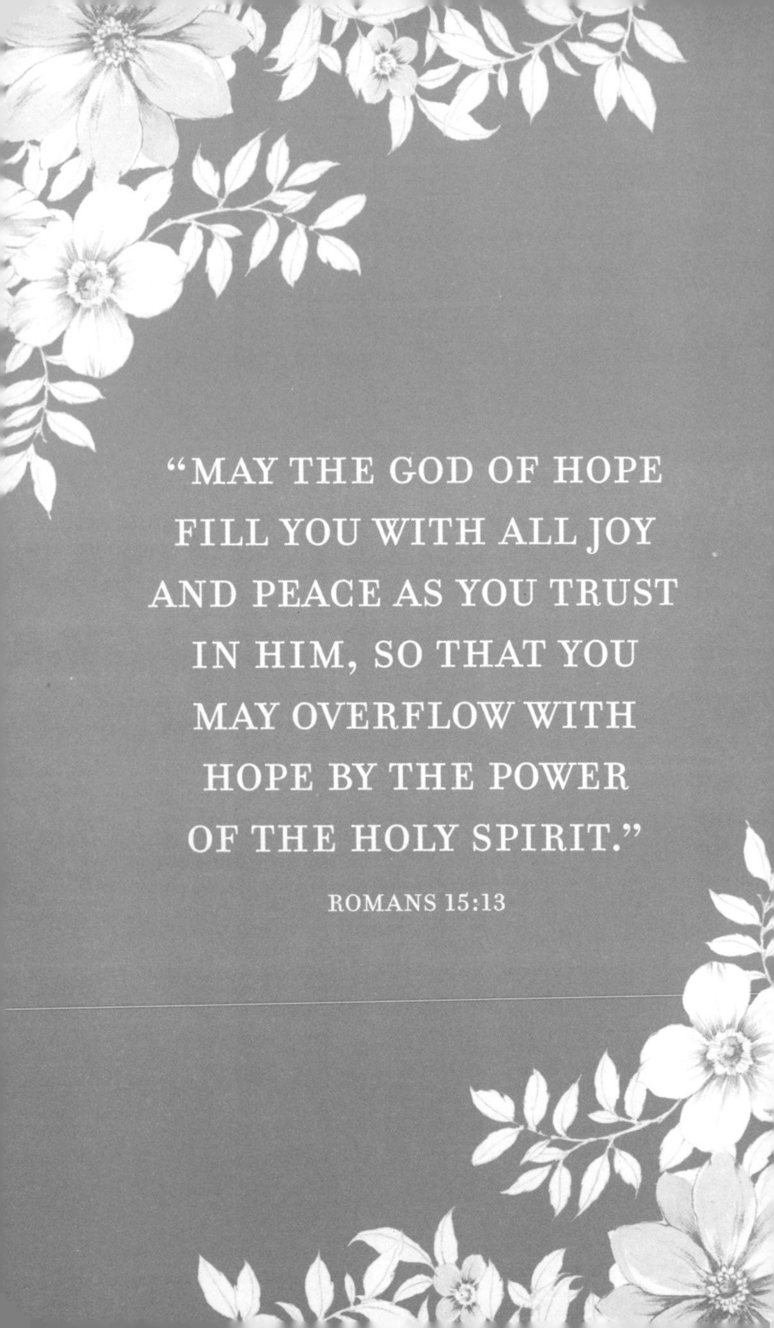

"MAY THE GOD OF HOPE
FILL YOU WITH ALL JOY
AND PEACE AS YOU TRUST
IN HIM, SO THAT YOU
MAY OVERFLOW WITH
HOPE BY THE POWER
OF THE HOLY SPIRIT."

ROMANS 15:13

46

From Doubt to Trust

"We have this hope as an anchor for the soul, firm and secure."

HEBREWS 6:19

Lord, I confess that my faith has wavered. My soul has been battered by the persistent, pelting rain of life. Your Word says that "the one who doubts is like a wave of the sea, blown and tossed by the wind" (James 1:6b). God, I don't want to be tossed about by the wind. I long to stand secure in my trust of You, the almighty One. Strengthen my faith, I pray.

When the storms come, give me the grace and supernatural stamina to cling to the anchor of hope that can only be found in You. You are my firm foundation, my only hope in life and death.

Thank You for promising that You will lose none of those who belong to You (see John 6:39), and that You will finish the work You have begun in me (see Philippians 1:6).

Amen

47

The Depths of Sorrow

"The Lord is close to the brokenhearted
and saves those who are crushed in spirit."

PSALM 34:18

Lord, my heart is broken and bleeding. I am filled with grief. I hardly have words to adequately express my sorrow. My spirit is crushed; I feel utterly deflated and defeated.

Your Word says You will never leave or forsake me, but I confess I'm struggling to sense Your presence with me. Help me to see glimpses of Your grace and feel the nearness of Your love.

In the midst of this dark, lonely valley, show me evidence of Your footprints next to mine. Bind up my wounds, I pray. I can't imagine healing from this pain, but I have to believe that it's possible for You to accomplish. Give me the stamina I need to endure this heartache.

In Your mercy, I am struck down but not destroyed. Thank You for being both powerful and compassionate enough to carry my hurting soul.

Amen

48

No Comparison

"I consider that our present sufferings are not worth comparing with the glory that will be revealed in us."

ROMANS 8:18

Lord, I need a perspective adjustment. I get so bogged down by the difficulty of my current circumstances, that it's hard to imagine better days beyond this moment.

Help me to remember that, even though it may not feel like it right now, these present sufferings are only temporary, and they are achieving a higher purpose.

Give me a vision for the glory that will soon be revealed in me at the second coming of Christ. Ignite my soul with a holy anticipation for eternity with You. Motivate me with the fuel I need to finish this race well, for Your glory.

There is truly no comparison between these finite struggles and the infinite joy I will soon know when I am with You.

Thank You for promising to keep me until the end. I depend wholly on Your sustaining grace and love.

Amen

A God Who Rejoices

"He will rejoice over you with gladness; He will quiet you by His love; He will exult over you with loud singing."

ZEPHANIAH 3:17B (ESV)

Lord, I confess that sometimes I am tempted to think of You as a harsh God who frequently dishes out punishment and discipline. I am plagued by the guilt of my sin, and I fear the consequences.

But Your Word reminds me that while You are a God of justice who grieves over sin, You also rejoice over me with gladness. I admit that it's hard for me to imagine You exulting over me with loud singing, but I believe it is true. Because of Jesus' work on the cross, I am covered by His blood and therefore acceptable in Your sight through faith.

I praise You for being a God who genuinely delights in His children. Thank You for offering me fullness of joy in Your presence (see Psalm 16:11).

Quiet me with Your love, I pray.

Amen

50

When You Feel Abandoned

"You have sorrow now, but I will see you again, and your hearts will rejoice, and no one will take your joy from you."

JOHN 16:22 (ESV)

Lord, I confess that my affections often lie with other people in my life more than You. I give portions of my heart away, and I am often let down and disappointed.

I feel alone, God. I trusted someone who was not trustworthy, and now I am paying the price. Forgive me for trying to find satisfaction in another. Reveal my idols and enable me to lay them aside in exchange for Your rule in my heart.

Bind up this wound with Your love, I pray. Only You can heal me from this hurt. Overwhelm me with Your tender mercy. Cause me to see You as more attractive and beautiful than anyone else. You alone can meet my needs and fulfill the desires of my heart.

Come, Lord Jesus. Be my source of constant, irrevocable, and living joy.

Amen

"THEREFORE DO NOT WORRY ABOUT TOMORROW, FOR TOMORROW WILL WORRY ABOUT ITSELF. EACH DAY HAS ENOUGH TROUBLE OF ITS OWN."

MATTHEW 6:34

51

A Difficult Diagnosis

"You will keep in perfect peace those whose minds are steadfast, because they trust in You."

ISAIAH 26:3

Lord, this diagnosis has rocked me to my core. I have no idea what the future holds. Give me the grace to endure the next steps, come what may.

Keep me in Your perfect peace. Help me to be steadfast in my faith, Lord. I feel so shaken by this news. Though it seems as if the ground beneath me is giving way, assure me that You are my firm foundation. You shall not be moved. You are my refuge; no matter what happens, I am safe in Your grip.

You are the great physician, the healer, the one who mends broken hearts and binds up wounds. But even if you choose not to heal in this life, Lord, give me an unwavering confidence in the complete healing that is promised in the life to come for those who trust in You.

Amen

52

The Truth about Worry

"Who of you by worrying can add a single hour to your life?"

LUKE 12:25

Lord, thank You for the reminder that my worries are frivolous and useless. I realize that worrying accomplishes nothing, yet it's so hard for me to stop. I've trained myself to fear, and I need Your help to overcome this unhelpful habit.

Show me how to take every thought captive and make it obedient to Christ (see 2 Corinthians 10:5). I know my fears and concerns are a sign of my lack of faith and trust. If I had full confidence in Your sovereignty, I would have no reason to worry. Increase my assurance of Your grace and provision, Lord. Forgive my unbelief. Help me to trust in Your perfect will.

You have already determined the sum of my years; You know every hair on my head (see Luke 12:7). Teach me to number my days, that I may gain a heart of wisdom and humility (see Psalm 90:12).

Amen

53

The Tenderness of God

"As a mother comforts her child, so will I comfort you."

ISAIAH 66:13A

Lord, You are a gentle and compassionate God. Unlike other religions in which their gods are far off and unknown, You care intimately about Your children.

Thank You for inviting me to call You "Abba, Father" (Romans 8:15). Thank You for desiring my good. Thank You for nurturing me with a holy tenderness.

Forgive me for the times I have sought comfort elsewhere. The solace I find in You cannot be found anywhere else. Your care has no comparison.

Thank You for promising comfort in Your Word. Even in the times when you feel far away from me, I know You are watching over me, carrying me, and sustaining me. Help me to trust in Your constant provision, especially in the moments when I cannot see Your hand at work.

Help me to silence the voices that tempt me to doubt Your goodness. There is no other love like Yours.

Amen

54

Jars of Clay

"But we have this treasure in jars of clay to show that this all-surpassing power is from God and not from us."

2 CORINTHIANS 4:7

Lord, I confess that sometimes I act as if I have superpowers. I try to do it all, to hold it all together. I pretend as if I'm indestructible and make every effort not to let the cracks in my armor be revealed. But the truth is, I am nothing without You. I can do nothing without You—not on the "good" days and especially not on the trying ones. You are my every breath.

Remind me that it's okay to let people see the cracks, because that's often when and where Your light shines through. Help me to embrace my weakness and Your strength. Use my story to glorify Your name.

Mold me into Your likeness, I pray. Cause this trial to shape me and refine me. Use me as Your humble instrument, for Your glory and honor.

Amen

55

For the Downcast Soul

"But You, O LORD, are a shield about me,
my glory, and the lifter of my head."

PSALM 3:3 (ESV)

Lord, my soul is downcast. I feel sad and discouraged more often than I feel happy or content. My burdens are weighing me down. I am struggling to see even a glimmer of hope in my situation. "How long must I take counsel in my soul and have sorrow in my heart all the day?" (Psalm 13:2a, ESV)

I feel tired all the time; it takes every ounce of energy I can muster just to get out of bed in the mornings and face a new day.

I need You to be the lifter of my head. "Answer me when I call to You... Give me relief from my distress; have mercy on me and hear my prayer" (Psalm 4:1). Help me to look up. Give me glimpses of Your hand at work in the midst of these difficult circumstances.

Amen

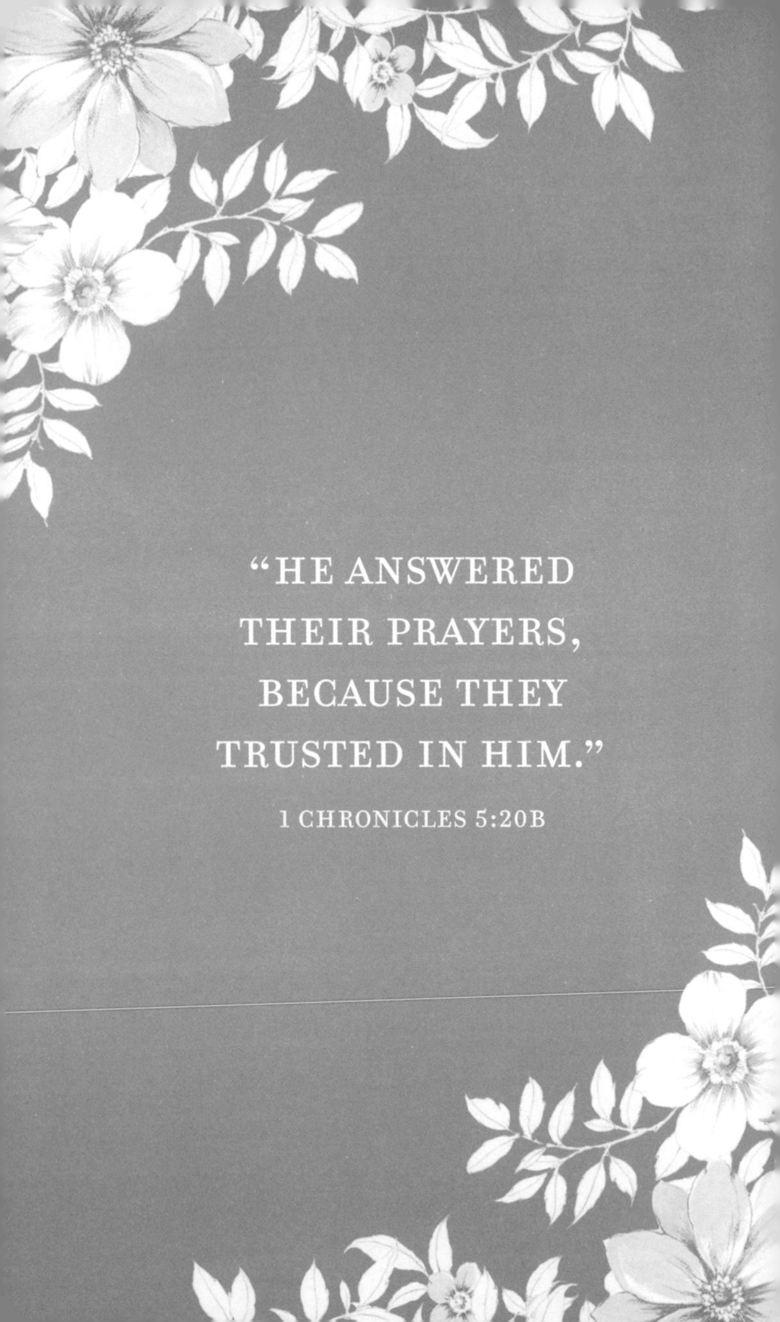
"HE ANSWERED
THEIR PRAYERS,
BECAUSE THEY
TRUSTED IN HIM."
1 CHRONICLES 5:20B

56

The Greatest of All

"He who is in you is greater than he who is in the world."

1 JOHN 4:4 (ESV)

Lord, sometimes it seems as if I cannot win. I feel defeated from every side. I am constantly losing battle after battle. The enemy continually makes life difficult for me.

Thank You for claiming the victory through Christ's death and resurrection. You have power and authority even over Satan. He needed permission from You to inflict hardship on Job (see Job 1:12). Though he bruised Your heel, You have crushed his head (see Genesis 3:15). You have already won. He may continue to roam the earth for a while, but a day is coming when You will put all Your enemies under the feet of Christ (see 1 Corinthians 15:24-26; Hebrews 10:13).

Increase my confidence in Your power. Teach me to speak truth to rebuke the Devil when He taunts me. You are greater than all, the almighty One in whom I delight.

Amen

In Times of Want

"Though the olive crop fails and the fields produce no food... yet I will rejoice in the Lord, I will be joyful in God my Savior."

HABAKKUK 3:17B–18

Lord, my circumstances are bleak. I am so needy. Like the apostle Paul, teach me "the secret of being content in any and every situation, whether well fed or hungry, whether living in plenty or in want" (Philippians 4:12b).

Thank You for Your example of feeding the birds of the air and clothing the grass of the field and Your promise that You will do even more for me (see Matthew 6:25–30). Help me to trust in Your faithful provision. Give me the grace not to worry about tomorrow (see Matthew 6:34).

Grant me a holy determination to practice sincere joyfulness in You because of who You are and all You have done for me through Christ. You are a good Father, and You have never let me down. Thank You.

Amen

58

Confronting Prejudice

"There is neither Jew nor Gentile, neither slave nor free, nor is there male and female, for you are all one in Christ Jesus."

GALATIANS 3:28

Lord, there is so much division in this world, and it only seems to be getting worse—even in Your church. It pains me to see brothers and sisters bickering on social media and in person, allowing conflict and differences of opinion to fracture relationships. Congregations have split, families no longer speak to one another, and Your name is dragged through the dirt.

I confess that I have contributed more harm than good. Reveal to me the places in my heart that hold prejudice, and cause me to repent. Forgive me, Lord, for the times I have sowed disunity rather than peace.

Father, You are the great unifier. You have broken down the dividing wall of hostility (see Ephesians 2:14). It's only through You that true and lasting peace will be achieved. Make us one, Lord—for Your name's sake.

Amen

59

The Fruit of Patience

"Wait for the Lord; be strong and take heart and wait for the Lord."

PSALM 27:14

Lord, I confess that I am not a patient person. In this world of instant gratification, I'm embarrassed to admit that I want what I want, and I want it now. And yet, Your Word tells me that patience is a fruit of the Spirit (see Galatians 5:22). I long to bear fruit for Your glory, Lord; help me to grow in this attribute.

It is especially challenging for me to wait on You during times of hardship, trial, and uncertainty. I want to know that everything is going to be okay. Remind me that You are working all things for the good of those who love You (see Romans 8:28), and that on the last day, everything will be far better than okay.

Lord, You are patient, forbearing, long-suffering, slow to anger. Fill me with Your Spirit, and help me to emulate You for Your glory.

Amen

In Times of Upheaval

"Peace I leave with you; My peace I give you… Do not let your hearts be troubled and do not be afraid."

JOHN 14:27

Lord, I cannot seem to settle my heart. Fears and worries consume my mind day and night. I am constantly fretting about countless variations of "What if?" It feels as if the world around me is falling apart. There is brokenness, pain, and sin everywhere I look. What will happen next?

Help me to remember these words You left for Your disciples and for me. Show me how to receive and embrace Your peace—not just with lip service, but with sincerity and trust. I pray, Lord, that Your peace would not be a temporary, fleeting feeling but that You would fill me with it. Push the fears out of my mind and heart, and consume me with Your everlasting peace instead. The comforts and distractions of this world are temporary; I need You and You alone.

Amen

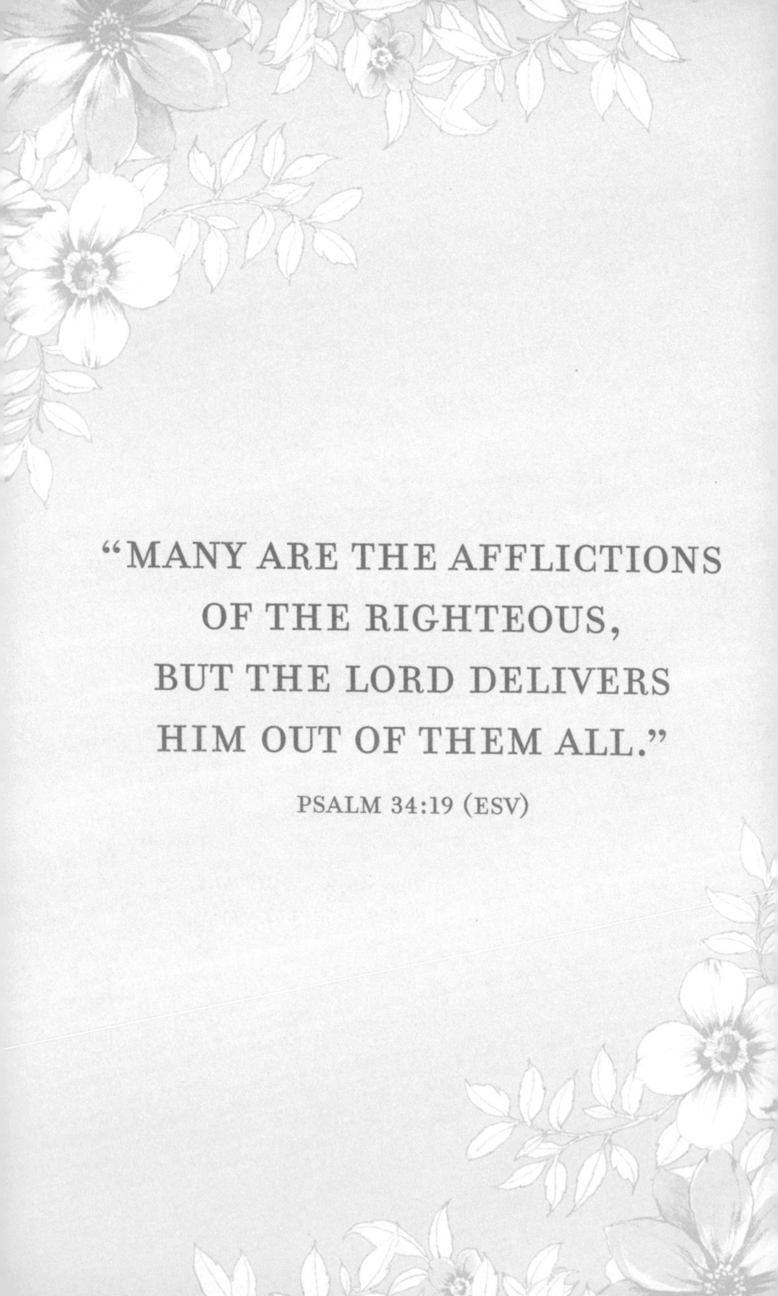

"MANY ARE THE AFFLICTIONS
OF THE RIGHTEOUS,
BUT THE LORD DELIVERS
HIM OUT OF THEM ALL."

PSALM 34:19 (ESV)

61

Overcoming Besetting Sin

*"For I do not do the good I want to do,
but the evil I do not want to do—this I keep on doing."*

ROMANS 7:19

Lord, I am a sinner. I fall down multiple times every day. I get so frustrated with myself; why do I continue to struggle with the same trespasses over and over again?

Thank You for being so patient and long-suffering with me. You are compassionate and merciful. I deserve nothing, and You give freely. Help me not to take Your grace for granted.

As long as I am in this body, I realize this will be an ongoing battle. I need Your Spirit to give me the supernatural strength to resist the temptations when they come. Thank You for promising to provide a way out (1 Corinthians 10:13).

Lord, I pray that You would give me an increasing distaste for the temporary pleasures of sin and an increasing appetite to serve and honor You.

Amen

The God Who Sees

"'You are the God who sees me.'"

GENESIS 16:13

Lord, there is so much injustice in this world. When I dwell on it, I feel despondent. Will it ever end? Wicked people seem to get away with immeasurable evil, most often at the expense of the innocent and oppressed.

I think about the story of Hagar in the Bible, the servant who was mistreated by her masters Abram and Sarai. After Sarai dealt harshly with her, Hagar fled (see Genesis 16:6). Then You appeared to Hagar in the wilderness and addressed her. "So she called the name of the Lord who spoke to her, 'You are a God of seeing,' for she said, 'Truly here I have seen Him who looks after me'" (Genesis 16:13 ESV).

Lord, thank You for being the God who sees me, who sees the injustices in this world. I praise You for being a just and holy God who cares for His people.

Amen

63

When a Loved One Is Ill

"And the peace of God, which surpasses all understanding, will guard your hearts and your minds in Christ Jesus."

PHILIPPIANS 4:7 (ESV)

Lord, my loved one is not well, and it's making me sick with worry. My whole body feels clenched up with anxious thoughts. I cannot still my mind. Day and night I wonder if the worst will happen. In this tense situation, I try to justify my fears as normal and rational. The thought of possessing peace in my heart at a time like this seems absurd. And yet, Your Word reminds me that the peace You offer surpasses all understanding. I cannot comprehend it. It is truly supernatural.

Father, I am desperate. Please fill me with this peace that can only come from You, the Prince of Peace. Guard my heart and my mind, and help me to dwell on truth instead of doubts and fears. Use Your divine comfort to show others how powerful You are.

Amen

The Pain of Betrayal

"Even my close friend, someone I trusted, one who shared my bread, has turned against me."

PSALM 41:9

Lord, I didn't realize I could hurt so deeply. The pain of betrayal is great. You know it intimately—infinitely more than I ever could.

I feel foolish, defeated, and numb. Fill the emptiness in my heart with Your gentle presence. Refresh my soul with Your tender compassion.

It baffles me that even though Jesus knew Judas would be the one to betray Him, He still offered him a place at the table, still fed him and nourished him. Teach me from the example of Christ. Make me gracious rather than bitter. Show me how to forgive with the same lavish forgiveness I have received from You.

Heal me with the assurance of Your love. Take these shards and make me whole. You are my constant companion. You will never betray me. Increase my trust in You alone, and use this heartbreak for Your glory.

Amen

65

The Strength of the Lord

"Be strong in the Lord and in the strength of His might."

EPHESIANS 6:10 (ESV)

Lord, I am weak. I cannot carry this burden on my own. I'm so tired from the ongoing trials in this dark valley. Every day I try to put one foot in front of the other, but my feet are heavy and the ground beneath me feels like sinking sand. I'm crying out to You for help.

I know I can't do this alone. I need You, God. Thank You for the gift of Your Holy Spirit. Thank You for offering me Your strength. It's the only way I can carry on. Give me the strength that I need to press on through this trial until the end.

You are the almighty One. There is no one more powerful than You.

Help me to rely on You and not myself. "For when I am weak, then I am strong" (2 Corinthians 12:10b).

Amen

"MY COMFORT IN
MY SUFFERING IS THIS:
YOUR PROMISE
PRESERVES MY LIFE."

PSALM 119:50

66

Even in Death

"When calamity comes, the wicked are brought down, but even in death the righteous seek refuge in God."

PROVERBS 14:32

Lord, You are a God of justice. Those who commit wicked acts and do not turn their hearts to you in this life will face consequences. But those who trust in Jesus Christ for their salvation will always find refuge in You—even in death.

Even if I don't see the outcomes I desire in this lifetime, Lord, help me to remember that You are my Savior, Redeemer, Protector, and Defender now and into the life to come. I may face pain and hardship for a little while, but my ultimate hope is anchored in something far deeper and more secure than this temporary earthly existence. I can run to You any time, knowing that You will guard me from anything that could harm my soul, because I have been purchased by the blood of Christ and nothing can snatch me from Your hand.

Amen

Wordless Groans

"For we do not know what to pray for as we ought, but the Spirit Himself intercedes for us with groanings too deep for words."

ROMANS 8:26B (ESV)

Lord, thank You for supplying my needs in every way imaginable. Even when I don't know what words to pray, You provide for me through the Holy Spirit's intervention and intercession on my behalf.

Thank You for the promise that Jesus Himself is interceding for me while He is at Your right hand in glory (Romans 8:34). I lack nothing as Your child.

You understand my anguish and agony. You know why it's hard for me to come up with words to use in prayer. Yet I know that You are the only one I can turn to, the only one who can bring about lasting change.

Thank You for hearing my heart and for receiving intercession from Jesus and the Holy Spirit when I don't know what to say or how to say it.

Amen

68

A Plea for Peaceful Sleep

"In peace I will lie down and sleep, for You alone, Lord, make me dwell in safety."

PSALM 4:8

Lord, I'm struggling to sleep. I lie awake at night and my thoughts torment me. I cannot calm my mind or my heart. My brain is a swirl of worries about what could be. Quiet me with Your love. Remind me that You are my refuge and my hiding place. Help me to feel your loving arms around me. Give me a sense of safety and peace in Your presence. Help me to use these hours of wakefulness for good.

Thank You for promising rest and security. Thank You for dwelling with me. Grant me a deep, abiding trust in You and Your faithful care over me. If I am safe in Your grip, what can man do to me? (See Psalm 56:11.) I praise You for finishing the work on the cross and claiming the victory over the enemy.

Amen

Resisting Revenge

"Do not be overcome by evil, but overcome evil with good."

ROMANS 12:21 (ESV)

Lord, my sinful nature is rearing up like a wild horse, eager to exact revenge on the person who has hurt me so deeply.

Help me to obey Your Word and never follow through on my desire for vengeance. Show me how to leave room for Your holy wrath. Remind me of Your admonition, "'It is mine to avenge; I will repay'" (Romans 12:19).

Instead, give me the grace to feed my enemy when they are hungry and give them something to drink when they are thirsty (see Proverbs 25:21). Strengthen me to take this unnatural response a step further to sincerely love and pray for my enemies. I know I can't do this on my own, Lord; You have to enable me through Your Spirit. Cause me to act in such a countercultural, supernatural way that others are led to question the source of my strength and find You.

Amen

The Prize of Perseverance

"Consider it pure joy...whenever you face trials of many kinds, because you know that the testing of your faith produces perseverance."

JAMES 1:2–3

Lord, I know Your Word says I should consider it pure joy whenever I face trials of many kinds, but I confess that pure joy is not an emotion that comes naturally to me when I'm in distress. Instead, I turn to worry and despair. And yet, it's usually during these times of hardship that You force me to my knees and show me just how much I need You.

Help me to gain the perspective that Charles Spurgeon possessed when he wrote, "I have learned to kiss the wave that throws me upon the Rock of Ages." Teach me how to be grateful for the circumstances that thrust me into Your arms. Use these trials, Lord, to strengthen my relationship with You and make me look more like Jesus—not only for my own benefit, but for Your glory.

Amen

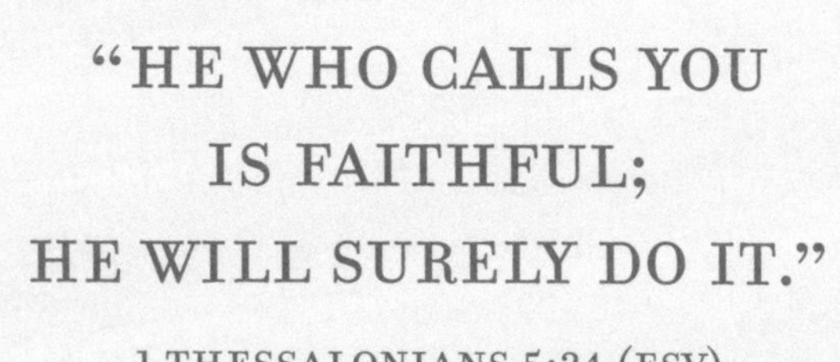

"HE WHO CALLS YOU
IS FAITHFUL;
HE WILL SURELY DO IT."

1 THESSALONIANS 5:24 (ESV)

For Times of Political Turmoil

"Some trust in chariots and some in horses,
but we trust in the name of the Lord our God."

PSALM 20:7 (ESV)

Lord, it seems as if the whole world is falling apart. Media coverage is full of reports of one disaster after the next. Uncertainties abound everywhere I look. Political strife has caused rifts that seem irreparable. Even Your church has succumbed to division.

You are the King of Kings and Lord of all. Though I may not see it from my limited vantage point, I know that You can turn the hearts of kings however You wish (see Proverbs 21:1). The entire creation belongs to You and is under Your authority and control. In You all things hold together (see Colossians 1:17).

No matter what happens, I know that You will remain on Your throne. You alone reign forever.

Teach me to pray for Your creation according to Your will and to trust in Your perfect rule.

Amen

72

Run the Race

"Let us run with perseverance the race marked out for us, fixing our eyes on Jesus, the pioneer and perfecter of faith."

HEBREWS 12:1B–2A

Lord, this trial has me so worn out; the thought of running a race seems daunting and entirely undesirable. And yet, I know that this whole life is a marathon, and I desire to run it well. Help me to find comfort in the truth that You have already marked out the course You planned for me. Show me how to pace myself for the long haul. Grant me the perseverance I need to press on until I reach the finish line.

Teach me how to focus not on reaching the end for the sake of relief, but to fix my eyes on Christ alone as my true hope and reward. Inspire me with His example. Lord, You gave me this gift of faith, and You alone can bring it to completion. I'm relying on You to carry me through.

Amen

73

Coping with Rejection

"If God is for us, who can be against us?"

ROMANS 8:31B (ESV)

Lord, rejection hurts. Every time. No matter how many times it happens, the sting is always the same. I wish I didn't care so much about what other people think, but I do—and I crave their approval. When my ideas, suggestions, or proposals get shot down, I take it personally, as if it's an attack against my identity.

Remind me that Your opinion is the only one that truly matters. Plant my feet on the solid foundation of Your Word. Ground me with my identity in Christ, as Your beloved child. Fix my mind on the truth that You are on my side, and You have already won. I need nothing and nobody besides You. Give me a holy confidence in who You are and who I am in You.

Heal the wounded parts of me with Your love, I pray. Cover me with the balm of Your grace.

Amen

Dealing with Depression

"You, Lord, are my lamp; the Lord turns my darkness into light."

2 SAMUEL 22:29

Lord, I am in a dark place. I cannot find my way. I need Your help. Please be a lamp to my feet and a light to my path (see Psalm 119:105).

I'm crying out to You in desperation. This place is so lonely and bleak.

Lord, I pray that You would turn this oppressive darkness into light. Your Word says that You are the light of the world (see John 8:12; 9:5). As Your child, I know I have Your light in me. Show me how to possess and shine the light of life.

My mind is continually dragging me down and leading me to despair. Cause me to cling to You as my anchor of hope.

Lead me out of these depths and back to solid ground. You are my firm foundation. In You alone do I place my trust for rescue and salvation.

Amen

75

When You Feel Excluded

"Therefore welcome one another as Christ has welcomed you, for the glory of God."

ROMANS 15:7 (ESV)

Lord, my heart hurts. Getting left out stings. The pain of being excluded is piercing and sharp. I know You can relate. You were separated from Your Son as He hung on the cross for my sins. I cannot imagine that kind of agony. In comparison, my discomfort is miniscule.

I know I've done the same thing to others in the past. Forgive me for my thoughtlessness, insensitivity, and unintentional sins. Open my eyes to others around me, especially those on the fringes and margins.

Lord, remind me that with You, I have not been left out. In Your Word, You say, "'You did not choose Me, but I chose you and appointed you so that you might go and bear fruit—fruit that will last'" (John 15:16). Thank You for choosing me.

Use this experience to help me bear fruit that will last.

Amen

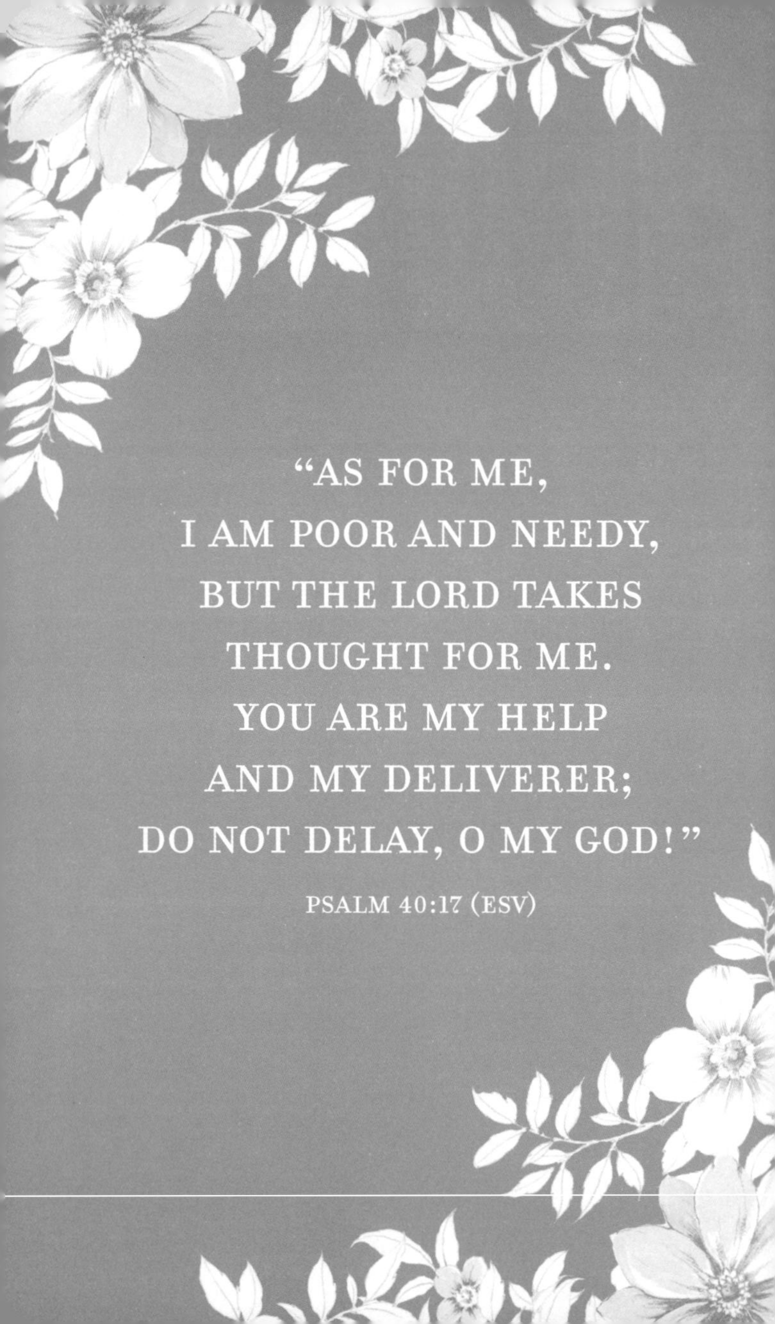
"AS FOR ME,
I AM POOR AND NEEDY,
BUT THE LORD TAKES
THOUGHT FOR ME.
YOU ARE MY HELP
AND MY DELIVERER;
DO NOT DELAY, O MY GOD!"
PSALM 40:17 (ESV)

The Battle Is the Lord's

"The Lord will fight for you; you need only to be still."

EXODUS 14:14

Lord, I confess that I often expend my own efforts before turning to You. Forgive me for not coming to You first. Remind me that my strivings get me nowhere in this life or the next. Calm my fears over what could be if I don't do something myself to prevent it.

Help me to be still and know that You are God (see Psalm 46:10). Slow me down and teach me to rest in You and Your ability and willingness to fight these battles on my behalf.

You alone are all-powerful and worthy to be praised. Thank You for going before me and shielding me from danger. Thank You for already claiming the victory through Your Son, Jesus Christ. Make my heart rejoice in Your triumph and find peace in the truth that the war has already been won. The enemy has been defeated. Praise the Lord.

Amen

Facing Terminal Illness

"For we know that if the earthly tent we live in is destroyed, we have a building from God, an eternal house in heaven, not built by human hands."

2 CORINTHIANS 5:1

Lord, I know that my days are numbered. I know that death comes to all of us—I just didn't expect it to come knocking so soon.

Facing the reality of the end brings such a vast array of thoughts and emotions. I confess that I have experienced flashes of doubt, fear, anger, sadness, grief, and more. Help me to lay these feelings at Your feet as an offering. Thank You for being big enough and strong enough to carry all of it. I pray that You would replace these burdens with joy, peace, contentment, and hope.

Thank You for the promise that You have prepared a place for me (John 14:2-3). Give me an eager anticipation for that eternal house where I can dwell in Your presence forever.

Amen

Peace Is a Person

"For He himself is our peace."

EPHESIANS 2:14A (ESV)

Lord, so often I have craved peace and sought it from the wrong places. I have tried my hardest to push worry away and muscle my mind and heart into a state of calm, but it never lasts. I have told myself if I could just trust You more, I would be less stressed, anxious, and afraid. Even when I have prayed for peace, I've often thought of it as a condition that You could impart to me. I didn't realize You already gave it to me in the form of a person—Your Son, Jesus Christ.

Help me to truly understand what it means that He Himself is my peace. Keep me from seeking calm or tranquility from external sources. Show me when I'm trying to establish a sense of peace through my own efforts. Teach me what it means to embrace Christ as my eternal peace and to find my rest in Him.

Amen

79

Unmatched Power

"David said to the Philistine, 'You come against me with sword and spear and javelin, but I come against you in the name of the Lord Almighty.'"

1 SAMUEL 17:45

Lord, I confess that sometimes I am afraid of the worldly attacks that come against me in various forms. Instead of standing firm in my faith, I am tempted to turn and run. I feel ill-equipped to do battle against my adversaries. I often forget the unmatched power that is accessible to me through Your name and Your Spirit, who dwells in me.

Give me a faith and confidence in You like David had in Your name and Your ability to overcome any weapon or foe. You are infinitely stronger than any force on this earth or in the spiritual realms. I worship You as the almighty One. Show me signs of Your magnificent power in my life, and help me to testify before others of Your immeasurable greatness. Strengthen my faith, I pray.

Amen

Hope in Times of Trouble

*"'In this world you will have trouble.
But take heart! I have overcome the world.'"*

JOHN 16:33B

Lord, I've heard people say that those who trust in You should not have trials in this life if their faith is strong enough. But in Your Word, You say the opposite. You say that I *should* expect trouble in this world. It's guaranteed. But that's not where the message ends.

Thank You for encouraging me to take heart. Even more, thank You for the work You did on the cross to defeat sin and overcome the world. In You I know I already have the victory because of Your sacrificial death and resurrection.

Keep my eyes focused on the end game. Lift my sight beyond these present challenges to eagerly anticipate what lies ahead when You return—eternity in Your presence. Help me to keep a right perspective of my current circumstances, knowing that they will soon end in exchange for glory with You.

Amen

"...WE REJOICE IN OUR SUFFERINGS, KNOWING THAT SUFFERING PRODUCES ENDURANCE, AND ENDURANCE PRODUCES CHARACTER, AND CHARACTER PRODUCES HOPE..."

ROMANS 5:3–4 (ESV)

81

When Life Feels Heavy

"'Come to Me, all you who are weary and burdened, and I will give you rest.'"

MATTHEW 11:28

Lord, I don't know how much longer I can go on like this. Sometimes life just seems too much for me to handle. I am weary and burdened.

Thank You for inviting me to come to You. I confess that I have been trying to do it all on my own. I have not turned to You or opened my hands to allow You to take the weight I am holding.

Father, help me to hand these burdens over to You and Your capable shoulders. Show me how to lay my troubles at the cross and entrust it all to You. Thank You for not only carrying my concerns, but for carrying me. Apart from You I can do nothing (see John 15:5). I am weak, but You are strong.

Thank You for promising rest—now and forever. Help me to rest in You.

Amen

Perseverance Under Trial

"Blessed is the one who perseveres under trial because, having stood the test, that person will receive the crown of life."

JAMES 1:12A

Lord, I confess that I have grown weary of this trial. My stamina to endure decreases by the day. I want to persevere, but I need Your help. I know that Your supply of power and strength never runs out. You are a generous God, able and willing to do immeasurably more than all I could ask or imagine (see Ephesians 3:20).

Grant me the grace I need to stand firm in my faith in the midst of this test. I long to maintain a testimony that gives glory and honor to You.

Remind me that this life is not the end; increase my desire for the life to come. Provide me with the strength I need to "press on toward the goal to win the prize for which God has called me heavenward in Christ Jesus" (Philippians 3:14).

Amen

In Times of Illness

"My flesh and my heart may fail, but God is the strength of my heart and my portion forever."

PSALM 73:26

Lord, I feel so miserable. With each morning that I wake, I am keenly aware of my own frailty. This earthly body is failing me. It feels as if it is deteriorating more and more every day. If ever I was tempted to think I was strong in my own strength, You remind me that it does not take much at all to bring me down.

On my own, I am feeble and weak. You alone are the source of my strength—physically, emotionally, mentally, and spiritually. Even though my body may fail, You will never fail me. You promise to uphold me and keep me until I get to spend eternity with you. Thank You for sustaining me.

Lord, help me to use my ailments and testimony to glorify Your name. I long for others to know Your amazing love.

Amen

His Grace Is Sufficient

"'My grace is sufficient for you, for My power is made perfect in weakness.'"

2 CORINTHIANS 12:9 (ESV)

Lord, help me to keep this phrase on repeat throughout each day: "His grace is sufficient. His grace is sufficient." So often, I grow frustrated trying to do it all on my own. I feel overwhelmed by pain and heartache. I am daily aware of my weaknesses and shortcomings.

Instead of hanging my head in embarrassment, show me how to boast in my weaknesses so that Your power might be made known through me. Use my failures and imperfections to glorify Yourself, I pray. Thank You for promising new mercies every morning.

Keep me from relying on other people or earthly things that cannot satisfy or provide for my needs. Protect me from depending on distractions instead of You. When everything else is stripped away, give me the ability to speak these words and believe them in my heart: "His grace is sufficient for me."

Amen

85

Past the Finish Line

*"I have fought the good fight,
I have finished the race, I have kept the faith."*

2 TIMOTHY 4:7 (ESV)

Lord, some days I feel as if I can't go on. My legs are so tired; my feet hurt from running this race. I want to finish strong and well for Your glory, but I'm so weary from these constant hurdles and obstacles. I'm running against the wind, and the pelting rain is in my eyes. I can't even see if I'm in the right lane.

Forgive me for trying to sprint in my own strength. Convict me of my desperate need for You. Your faithfulness is my adrenaline. Your grace is the blood in my veins. Teach me to pace myself according to Your will.

Energize me with a fresh dose of Your mercy. Breathe fresh wind at my back, Lord; propel me forward in Your strength. Spur me on with the urge to hear You say, "Well done, good and faithful servant."

Amen

“HE GIVES STRENGTH
TO THE WEARY AND
INCREASES THE POWER
OF THE WEAK.”

ISAIAH 40:29

My Faithful Shepherd

"Even though I walk through the valley of the shadow of death, I will fear no evil, for You are with me; Your rod and Your staff, they comfort me."

PSALM 23:4 (ESV)

Lord, thank You for being such a faithful Shepherd. Even though this valley is so very dark, Lord, I can sense Your presence with me. Thank You for quelling my fears with Your nearness.

The density of this shadow is hampering my vision. Like a lost, wandering sheep, I need Your rod of correction and Your gentle staff to guide me back to the right path. Thank You for caring enough about me to find me and rescue me. You are my Comforter and my trustworthy guide.

Give me the stamina and perseverance to keep walking in this unlit place. Remind me that the light of Christ dwells within me. Show me how to shine Your light not only for my own benefit, but to help others in this valley as well.

Amen

Temporary Troubles

"For our light and momentary troubles are achieving for us an eternal glory that far outweighs them all."

2 CORINTHIANS 4:17

Lord, this trial feels anything but light or momentary. The burden is great; my shoulders are weighed down and hunched over. It feels as if this difficult situation has been dragging on and lingering forever. Yet Your Word reminds me that not only are these troubles of mine temporary, they also serve a greater purpose that I cannot even fathom.

Give me Your eternal perspective, Lord. Bolster my endurance and stamina by helping me set my mind on things above, not on earthly things (see Colossians 3:2). Instill a deeper sense of perseverance in me by showing me the ultimate goal of everlasting glory with You. Grant me a longing to be in Your presence, and use that longing to help me carry on in Your grace and strength through this challenging time. Give me patience until You return or call me home.

Amen

88

You Supply All My Needs

"You will drink from the brook, and I have directed the ravens to supply you with food there."

1 KINGS 17:4

Lord, You have complete control over all creation. Even the birds listen to You and obey Your commands. Just as You promised Elijah in the verse above, "The ravens brought him bread and meat in the morning and bread and meat in the evening, and he drank from the brook" (1 Kings 17:6).

You provide in miraculous, extravagant ways. You know exactly what I need and when I need it. Help me to banish all fears of not having enough. Increase my trust in Your abundant provision. You are so good to me; I don't deserve Your love. Thank You for caring for me morning, noon, and night.

Show me how I can take what I've been given and offer it back to You and Your people. Help me to reflect Your lavish generosity through my interactions with others.

Amen

He Will Restore You

"After you have suffered a little while, the God of all grace, who has called you to His eternal glory in Christ, will Himself restore, confirm, strengthen, and establish you."

1 PETER 5:10 (ESV)

Lord, thank You for the comforting power of Your Word. I'm so grateful for Your faithful promises to Your children. I praise You for sustaining me with Your guarantee of the life to come.

Thank You for the reminder that these sufferings are only temporary. Grant me the strength to endure them to the end. You are indeed the God of all grace. Keep me in awe of Your character.

Thank You for calling me to Yourself. I cannot imagine trying to do life without You. I'm so grateful for the assurance that one day soon, You will restore, confirm, strengthen, and establish me by Your grace.

Give me an undying yearning to experience eternal glory with Christ. Use me and my circumstances to draw others to Yourself, I pray.

Amen

90

Facing Opposition

"The name of the Lord is a strong tower;
the righteous man runs into it and is safe."

PROVERBS 18:10 (ESV)

Lord, thank You for being my faithful defender. Thank You for providing a safe refuge where I can hide away. Thank You for promising to protect me. There is no stronger ally or advocate than You. I feel peace in Your impenetrable arms.

When I am facing opposition, I know I can call on Your name, and You will rescue me. Increase my faith and erase my fears. Grow my confidence in You and Your unmatched power.

Give me the boldness to tell the world about who You are and what You have done. Use my story to strengthen the faith of others and lead them to trust in You. You are mighty to save. You have already defeated the greatest enemies of all—Satan, sin, and death. Thank You for the gift of salvation and the promised hope of eternal protection in Your presence.

Amen

"FOR I AM THE
LORD YOUR GOD
WHO TAKES HOLD OF
YOUR RIGHT HAND
AND SAYS TO YOU,
DO NOT FEAR;
I WILL HELP YOU."

ISAIAH 41:13

91

To the Very End

*"Having loved His own who were in the world,
He loved them to the end."*

JOHN 13:1B (ESV)

Lord, You sent Your one and only Son into the world, and He demonstrated the greatest love of all by sacrificing Himself for the sins of many. And yet, His death on the cross was not His only expression of love. The Scriptures record numerous stories of His lavish love for His people while He walked the earth and how "He loved them to the end." Even when they betrayed Him. Even when they handed Him over to death.

I can't see the finish line of this trial, Lord, and I've failed You so many times. I have betrayed You more times than I can count. Yet I'm clinging to the promise that You will love me to the end, whenever that may be. Thank You for Your enduring faithfulness and long-suffering with me, and for committing to love me and sustain me now and always.

Amen

The Source of My Strength

"The Sovereign Lord is my strength; He makes my feet like the feet of a deer, He enables me to tread on the heights."

HABAKKUK 3:19

Lord, my strength comes from You. When I feel tired and weary, You enable me to go on. I long to run this race well, God—for Your glory, not my own. Some days I'm not sure I can take another step, but You are faithful to give me the supernatural grace and energy I need to persevere.

You carry me to heights I didn't know were possible. Give me boldness to testify of the source of my strength. Keep me from claiming any credit for myself; everything You allow me to accomplish is purely by Your mercy and provision.

I realize this life is not a sprint, but a marathon. This is not the first or last trial I will face. Continue to grant me endurance until I reach the finish line, I pray.

Amen

Soon and Very Soon

"He will wipe every tear from their eyes. There will be no more death or mourning or crying or pain, for the old order of things has passed away."

REVELATION 21:4

Lord, I long for the day when there will be no more death or mourning or crying or pain. There are so many heartaches and hardships in this life; sometimes the grief feels too great to bear. I know You understand; Your Son experienced infinitely more during His time on this earth. I can't imagine the atrocities He endured on the cross, separated from You, bearing the sins of Your people.

Thank You for making it possible for me to hope for a perfect eternity with You. I praise You for the promise of a resurrection, of a new heavens and a new earth. Show me how to wait well. Give me a supernatural patience to endure the ongoing heartaches until You return or call me home.

Come, Lord Jesus.

Amen

94

The Promise of His Presence

"Do not fear, for I am with you; do not be dismayed,
for I am your God. I will strengthen you and help you;
I will uphold you with My righteous right hand."

ISAIAH 41:10A

Lord, so many times in the Scriptures when You tell Your people not to fear, You follow that command with the promise of Your presence. The fact that You are always with us is the reason we should not be afraid.

Thank You for the surety of Your promises. There is no shadow of doubt in Your words—You *are* with me, You *are* my God, You *will* strengthen me, You *will* help me, You *will* uphold me. You have done it, and You will continue to do it.

Father, forgive me for my feeble faith, for the moments and days when my trust falters. When I am tempted to be afraid, help me to sense Your presence with me as the ultimate source of comfort.

Amen

95

Press On

"Let us not grow weary of doing good,
for in due season we will reap, if we do not give up."

GALATIANS 6:9 (ESV)

Lord, I am weary. I am tired. It feels as if I've been enduring this trial for so very long. When will it end, God? And yet I realize that life is going on all around me in spite of my hardship. I confess that I have been particularly inward focused, concentrating on my own pain and neediness.

Help me to turn my gaze outward and upward. Show me how I can use my pain, my gifts, and my time for good—for the good of others and for the glory of Your name. Give me the stamina to serve others when I'm feeling drained and depleted. Grant me the patience and perseverance to carry out Your will for my life. Equip me with Your Spirit, and help me not to give up. Use me as Your instrument, I pray.

Amen

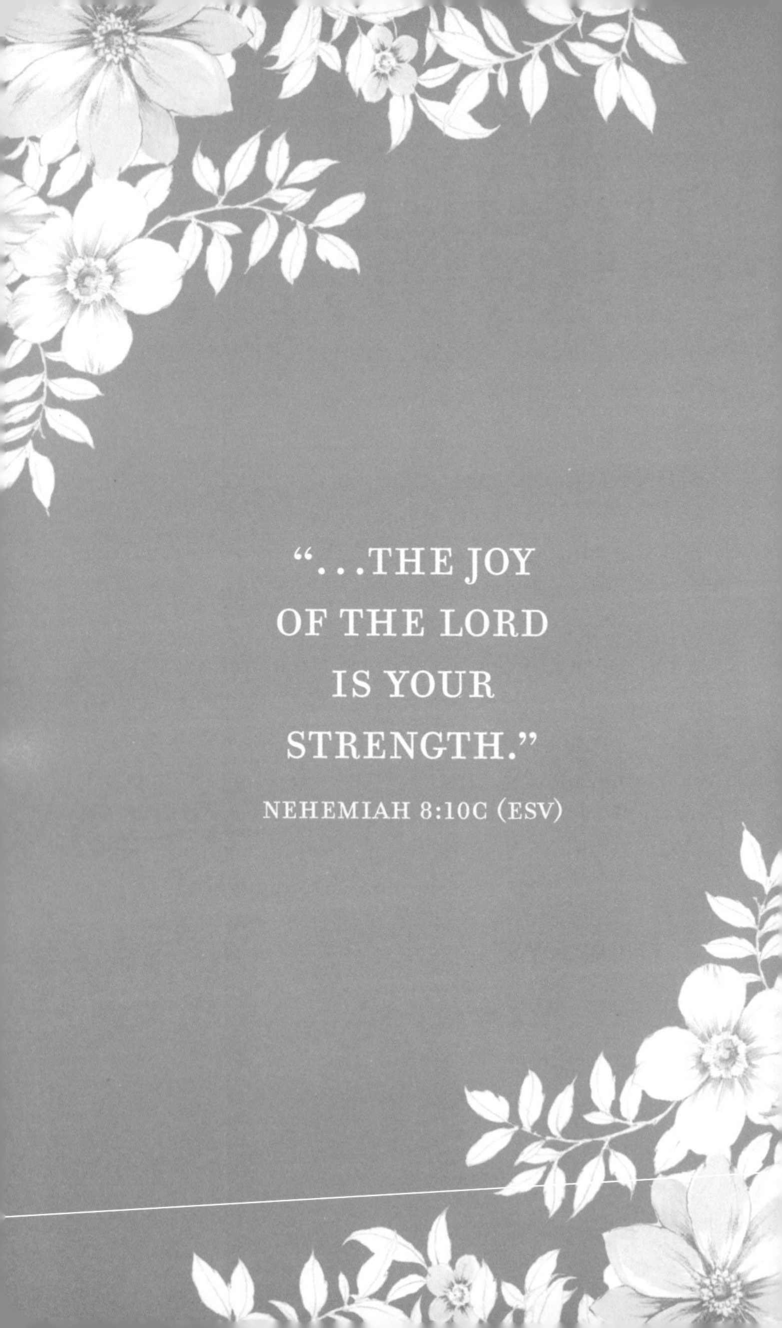
"...THE JOY
OF THE LORD
IS YOUR
STRENGTH."
NEHEMIAH 8:10C (ESV)

96

He Will Finish the Work

"He who began a good work in you will carry it on to completion until the day of Christ Jesus."

PHILIPPIANS 1:6B

Lord, I confess that sometimes I fear my faith will fail—especially when it's being tested by difficult circumstances. I am prone to wander. I seek solace and peace from places and people other than You. I fall down multiple times each day.

Thank You for promising to hold me fast. Thank You for never letting me go. Thank You for picking me up when I fall. Thank You for Your sustaining grace. Thank You for promising to carry me across the finish line, no matter how bruised or exhausted I may be when I get there.

Father, empower me with Your daily sustaining grace to persevere and keep running this marathon. Help me to look forward to the day when I finish the race and You welcome me into glory, where there will be no more hardship or pain.

Amen

97

Always and Only Faithful

"Not one word has failed of all the good promises He gave through his servant Moses."

1 KINGS 8:56B

Lord, You are amazing. Nothing compares with You. From the beginning of time, You have had a perfect plan that You continue to carry out and fulfill with each passing day.

Your Word is true. Every promise that You made, You have kept. The word "faithful" seems inadequate to describe Your greatness and Your unblemished precision to do exactly what You say You will do.

Lord, by your Spirit, remind me of your wondrous acts throughout history to bolster my own faith today. I confess that at times I doubt Your ability to intervene in my situation. I question Your plan for my life and whether it is really good. When I'm struggling with day-to-day challenges, my view of Your glory becomes clouded with doubt.

Enhance my vision of Your goodness, Lord. Fortify my trust in Your promises. Renew my anticipation for Your return.

Amen

98

Blessed Are the Steadfast

"We consider those blessed who remained steadfast... You have seen the purpose of the Lord, how the Lord is compassionate and merciful."

JAMES 5:11 (ESV)

Lord, You are full of compassion. You are abundant in mercy. You give me so much—more than I can measure. Forgive me for dwelling on the negative, for complaining about what I don't have, for grumbling about my circumstances.

My faith is feeble and fickle. Cause me to be steadfast in my devotion to You, God. I long to be faithful to You, Lord, but I know I can't do it without Your Holy Spirit and sustaining grace.

Give me a testimony that brings You all the praise and honor. Grant me the patience to wait for Your purposes to unfold in the midst of this hardship. Remind me of Your unfailing attributes and divine character when I'm tempted to waver. Help me to cling to the anchor of hope that is found in You alone.

Amen

99

Lead Me Home

"You have led in Your steadfast love the people whom You have redeemed; You have guided them by Your strength to Your holy abode."

EXODUS 15:13 (ESV)

Lord, You are my leader. I will follow You wherever You go. Forgive me for the times I have strayed from Your will for my life. Keep me close to You, I pray.

Thank You for being a gracious leader who leads with steadfast love. You embody gentleness and patience.

Thank You for the precious gift of redemption. You bought me with a price, and I am so grateful for Your costly rescue and salvation.

Thank You for guiding me by Your strength and not my own feebleness. You are my rock and my foundation.

Thank You for leading me step by step, moment by moment, to Your holy abode. Though this trial is burdensome, Your mercies are new every morning. Give me patience to persevere. I long for the day when I will be in Your presence.

Amen

Eternal Comfort

"May our Lord Jesus Christ Himself, and God our Father, who loved us and gave us eternal comfort...comfort your hearts."

2 THESSALONIANS 2:16–17 (ESV)

Lord, I confess that I often focus on the lack of comfort I am currently feeling. My vision is limited to this moment and the circumstances right in front of me. It's hard to see beyond this present darkness.

Help me to remember that the comfort You offer is eternal. Lift my eyes to see past the horizon to the life to come. Teach me to set my mind on things above.

Thank You for giving me a hope that is immeasurably greater than any temporary, earthly remedy. Your consolation is far superior to any source of solace I might find elsewhere.

Grant me the grace to dwell on Your character over and above my current condition. Instill Your gift of hope in my heart, and use that everlasting comfort to establish the work of my hands for Your glory alone.

Amen

101

Even to the End

"For this God is our God for ever and ever;
He will be our guide even to the end."

PSALM 48:14

Lord, there is none like You. All of the other so-called deities are impersonal, far off, and unreliable. You are the most faithful being who ever existed. You never give up on Your children. Even when I am faithless, You remain faithful, for You cannot deny Yourself (see 2 Timothy 2:13).

The journey feels long and arduous, God. So often I wander from Your path, blinded by temptations and my own weaknesses and sins. Thank You for being a faithful Shepherd who continually seeks, finds, and restores Your sheep.

Give me the grace to finish this race well. I admit my desperate need for You; thank You for sending Your Son to save me and Your Spirit to sustain me. I love You, Lord.

I praise You and worship You for promising to be my guide even to the end.

Amen

"NOW THE ONE WHO
HAS FASHIONED US
FOR THIS VERY
PURPOSE IS GOD,
WHO HAS GIVEN US
THE SPIRIT AS A DEPOSIT,
GUARANTEEING
WHAT IS TO COME."

2 CORINTHIANS 5:5

About the Author

Kate Motaung is the author of the memoir, *A Place to Land: A Story of Longing and Belonging*, and co-author of *Influence: Building a Platform that Elevates Jesus (Not Me)*.

She is the host of the Five Minute Friday Writing Community and owner of Refine Services, a business that offers editing services.

Kate grew up on the shores of Lake Michigan before spending ten years living in Cape Town, South Africa. She and her South African husband have three young adult children and currently live in West Michigan. Connect with Kate at katemotaung.com or fiveminutefriday.com.